How to Live in the Kingdom of God

HOW TO LIVE IN THE KINGDOM OF GOD

Challenge of the 21st Century

Richard Rundell

Writers Club Press
San Jose New York Lincoln Shanghai

How to Live in the Kingdom of God
Challenge of the 21st Century

Writers Club Press
an imprint of iUniverse.com, Inc.

For information address:
iUniverse.com, Inc.
5220 S 16th, Ste. 200
Lincoln, NE 68512
www.iuniverse.com

ISBN: 0-595-17610-0

Printed in the United States of America

CONTENTS

ACKNOWLEDGMENTS

I wish to thank my pastor, Gary Parson, of Redemption Life Tabernacle in Haskell, Oklahoma, for his consultation and help in writing this book.

To Jim Lockmiller, our associate pastor, for his input and review of the manuscript, I voice an expression of appreciation.

My gratitude to the members of our local church who continue to encourage me in my writing endeavors.

I thank Earl Moore for his review of the manuscript and writing the Foreword of the book.

My appreciation extends to Kathie Nee Scriven for her professional and expert job of editing the manuscript and for her consultation.

FOREWORD

By
Minister Earl L. Moore
P.O. Box 33168
Indianapolis, IN 46203-0168

The Epistle unto the Hebrews in Chapter 12, verse 28 declares an important truth that not very many bible students have given the proper consideration unto, "Wherefore we receiving a kingdom which cannot be moved, let us have grace, whereby we may serve God acceptable with reverence and godly fear."

This being a God given, new covenant fact, it then becomes of utmost necessity to learn as much s possible about this Kingdom that has already been given unto us.

The author, Richard W. Rundell, has made an in depth study into many facets concerning this kingdom. The revelation truths of this writing can become a faith building factor. It can also help Bible believers to better comprehend and get a greater understanding of the present inheritance and divine privileges of this glorious kingdom that are available unto them by the Lord Jesus Christ.

I believe this book will prove to be a real spiritual blessing for all who will take time to read and study the truths written herein. Whether the reader totally agrees with every detail of this book, the paramount truths revealed herein are truly worthy of your sincere consideration.

INTRODUCTION

So much of the world asks, "How long till we see the Kingdom of God?" Will it come in the near future? Must we wait until Jesus appears in person? Or has the Kingdom been established already? Jesus said, the Kingdom of God comes not by observation. By observation would mean you could see the Kingdom with your natural eyes or perceive it with your natural understanding.

This book, from the scriptures, addresses these issues as well as what, where, when and why concerning the Kingdom. What is more important, this book discusses, for each reader, how to live and walk victoriously day by day in the Kingdom—in this life.

At the time Jesus began His earthly ministry, His followers thought He would set up an earthly kingdom and subdue the rule that the Romans had over them. They envisioned their worst enemy was on the outside. As Jesus taught so well, instead, their enemy was the sin of Adam manifesting within them.

Today we find a similar dilemma. People just sit and wait, looking for the Kingdom of God to come and rule over the crime, violence, wars, corruption, illegal drugs, abortion, and the other ills of society, the enemies outside ourselves. The Kingdom of God however, must begin to rule in the hearts and lives of the deliverers, the leaders and members of the Kingdom. The Christian must grasp the truths of the Kingdom and allow such truths to reign in their everyday lives. What did the Apostle Paul mean, "Christ in you the hope of glory?" This book, by the Scriptures, confronts this question.

CHAPTER 1

▼

WHAT AND WHERE IS THE KINGDOM OF GOD?

What is the Kingdom of God?

Much confusion seems to exist in the body of Christ today as to what constitutes the Kingdom of God. Some appear to believe that all references to the Kingdom refer to heaven. In what is commonly called the Lord's prayer, however, Jesus said, "Thy Kingdom come, thy will be done in earth, as it is in heaven." (Matt 6:10) Or we might re-phrase His declaration by saying, "Thy will be done in the earthly or natural realm as it is in the heavenly or spiritual realm." Therefore, the Kingdom does not confine itself to a heavenly realm.

Remember that Jesus declared, "Behold, the Kingdom of God is within you." (Luke 17:21). Due to a misunderstanding of this verse, some people regard the Kingdom as all spiritual. We'll discuss this verse later.

Others quote John 18:36, "My kingdom is not of this world" to postpone the reality of the kingdom until the distant future. The word "world" from the above verse comes from the Greek word *"kosmos,"* meaning arrangement, order or system. The solar system, society, government, finance, education, commerce, industry, the field of physics and chemistry, and even the underworld operate by certain laws or systems. But all systems that don't originate from the mind of Christ are of the world. Jesus never denied His Kingdom was to be set up on earth, but He emphasized that His Kingdom was higher in origin and purpose than the present Roman kingdom or any kingdom that men might set up in the future. His Kingdom would be an entirely different type of order or system.

What are the ingredients of a Kingdom? They include (1). A king, one who rules with authority (John 1:49; Matt. 28:18-20); (2) The king's court, such as Prime Ministers, and governors (Rev. 5:10; 20:6); (3) A territory (Ps. 2:8; Matt. 6:10), (4). Laws or principles of living including a form of worship (Matt. 5:1-8:1); (5) Subjects or citizens who are subject to the law of the Kingdom (Deut. 4:40; Eph. 2:19; Phil. 3:20), and (6) Life style of the subjects (Isa. 60:1-5; John 10:10; 11:25; Rom. 5:21; 8:18). The king's court in the Kingdom of God (No. 2) consists of the leadership order, the five-fold ministry or the Melchizedec Priesthood. (Eph. 4:11-12)

The Kingdom of God contains more than a condition of the heart. It includes the sovereign rule of God, along with those appointed to rule with Him, and manifested in the person and work of Jesus Christ. This Kingdom brings forth a people over whom Christ reigns and operates as a realm in which the power of His reign is realized. "And hast made us unto our God kings and priests: and we shall reign on the earth." (Rev. 5:10 KJV)

The Kingdom of God includes the extension of God's kingly rule or dominion in the earth. It's the territory over which a **king** and His court rules and reigns. In God's primary plan and purpose for the Kingdom, His rule and domain extends not only to the earth, but also to the entire universe.

Quoting from *The Kingdom and the Power* by Peter J Leithart concerning the authority of Jesus Christ, we read, "Christ claimed all authority in heaven and earth (Matt. 28:18-20). Authority means the right to be obeyed. To say that Jesus has authority means that when He speaks He has an absolute right to be heard. His Word is law. Jesus is exalted as the covenant King, and along with His promises, He makes demands. All people everywhere are commanded to repent and turn to Him in trust and obedience and swear covenant loyalty to Him (Acts 6:7; 17:30). This was Jesus' central message while on earth: "*Repent*, for the kingdom of heaven is at hand" (Matt. 4:17, emphasis added)."

We read in Psalm 110: 1-2, "The LORD (YHVH) said unto my Lord (Jesus), Sit thou at my right hand, until I make thine enemies thy footstool. The LORD shall send the rod of thy strength out of Zion: rule thou in the midst of thine enemies." To "sit" here means to dwell in a position of authority, in this case, over our enemies. Whereas the enemies of the people of Israel in the Bible were natural enemies, our enemies today are spiritual. Other people aren't our enemies but the spirits that work in them and operate through our own carnal mind. Such spirits try to drag us into bondage into the law of sin and death. These spiritual enemies include the works of the flesh, our attitudes, fear, doubt and unbelief.

Verse 4 in the same Psalm states, "The LORD hath sworn, and will not repent, Thou art a priest for ever after the order of Melchizedek." This verse speaks of a priestly order to rule in the Kingdom. We see that Psalm 110 is a picture of the (true) Church coming forth, able to control its desires.

Wherever Jesus is Lord and King, the Kingdom of God prevails. This is the purpose and will of God. It prevails here and now, not just in the future nor for another people. "For he is not a Jew, which is one outwardly; neither is that circumcision, which is outward in the flesh: But he is a Jew, which is one inwardly; and circumcision is that of the heart, in the spirit, and not in the letter; whose praise is not of men, but of God" (Rom. 2:28-29).

This means that the Kingdom functions not only for the natural Jew but also for all mankind—every race and nation of people. The Jew, however, as well as the Gentiles, must come into the Kingdom through Jesus Christ. All are under sin. "What then? Are we better than they (the Jew)? Not at all. For we have previously charged both Jews and Greeks that they are all under sin." (Rom. 3:9 NKJV) It is through faith in the blood of Jesus Christ that we receive righteousness for the remission of our sins. (Rom. 3:25)

The Kingdom prevails when man submits to God and when man recognizes God's reign. The Kingdom likewise refers to God's sovereign rule in the universe, through the entry of God's Anointed One—the prophesied Messiah, the One who would not only be Savior, but King of all mankind. God promised this hope to all flesh. (Isa. 9:6-7; 11:10; 40:5) "And it shall come to pass in the last days, says God, That I will pour out of My Spirit on **all flesh...**" (Acts 2:17)

In the Old Testament economy people obeyed the laws mainly because of the consequences of disobedience, but under the new covenant, the subjects of the Kingdom of God willingly submit to Christ and obey Him from their heart. Let us quote from *The Prophetic Community* by Bishop Earl Paulk in regard to these laws and Christ: p. 7, "When Jesus came though, He wrote the laws of God on the people's hearts. Then people obeyed because they wanted to, because they loved the King who gave the laws."

In the culture of the time of Jesus, people considered the poor as being abandoned by God and poverty the result of sin and corruption. Furthermore, natural calamities people regarded as punishment from God. In the parable of the leaven (Matt. 13:33), the woman, a symbol of one ritually unclean, takes leaven, a symbol of corruption, and places it in three measures of meal. They would ask (we might also ask) Jesus, how can the Kingdom of God, that which is supposed to be holy, be compared to corruption. The Jewish religion of that time identified everyday life with corruption while temple rituals and feasts with the sacred. Jesus dispels this notion, teaching here and in other parables about the Kingdom that the Kingdom of God has much to do with our everyday life while in contrast the temple and its rituals is no longer the place to find the Kingdom. We are not doing away with corporate worship but with much ritual that originated in the pagan world. Remember Jesus told the women at the well, we no longer worship God in this mountain (geographical location, creation of God) or in Jerusalem (in some building, creation of man) but in Spirit. (John 4:21-23). The Samaritans worshipped Jacob's well (set up a monument) while the Jews worshipped the synagogue and its rituals (set up a monument to their religion).

In the parable of the publican and the Pharisee, Jesus points out that the Kingdom of God is no longer just in the temple in the self righteous Pharisees but is found outside the temple in the secular area, in the humility of the publicans. Thus, the sacred has moved to outside the temple to our everyday lives in the secular world while in the temple, we may find the unholy self-righteous.

In the parable of the lost coin, the woman called her friends and rejoiced over finding, not a pot of gold, but the lost coin. In a like manner, in the parable of the lost sheep, the man rejoiced over finding the one lost sheep, just as there is joy in heaven (the spiritual realm) when one sinner repents, more than over the ninety nine just persons. (Luke 15:4-9). Likewise in the Kingdom of God we experience not just the spectacular, but we find God working in our everyday lives. Yes, if we function under the anointing of Jesus Christ, we will also witness miracles, for that same power is within us that raised Jesus from the dead.

The Kingdom is a Territory

When Jesus spoke of the Kingdom of God, He spoke not of a geographical area like the country of Israel or the temple or some place off in the sky. Nor did He speak of a political entity, such as the nation of Israel.

The concept of God's Kingdom having dominion, however, over a specific area on earth began with Abraham. "Now the LORD had said unto

Abram, Get thee out of thy country, and from thy kindred, and from thy father's house, unto a land that I will show thee:" (Gen. 12:1)

God also gave promises concerning the land of Canaan to Isaac (Gen. 26:3) and to Jacob (Gen. 28:13). Later, in the time of Moses, the boundaries of the land were defined as stretching "...from the wilderness and Lebanon, from the river, the river Euphrates, even unto the uttermost sea shall your coast be." (Deut. 11:24)

The land of Canaan speaks of a type of our body and a type of the higher Christian life, to be won by spiritual warfare. Our spirit was saved by the blood of Jesus Christ while He is now in the process of saving our soul (mind, will and emotions) through the Holy Spirit (2 Cor. 1:10; 1 Pet. 1:9, 22; Rom. 12:2). Just as Canaan had to be possessed, our body is the territory we need to possess.

We know both the Old and New Testaments are filled with types and shadows of the reality of today (Heb. 8:5; 10:1). For example, the Passover lamb was a type of Jesus Christ, the Lamb of God, while the tabernacle in the wilderness discloses a type of present believers. The pilgrimages of Israel reveal a type of the Christian life.

Where is the Kingdom of God?

We find the Kingdom of God not out in the sky, but in the earth. We are that earth, our very being: spirit, soul and body. Heaven must come and manifest itself in the earth **in a people**. That is, the elements of the heavenly or spiritual realm must manifest in the earth, in a people in their everyday lives. When we speak of heaven here, we don't refer to a geographical place but a condition. (John 3:13). Thus, the gospel and principles of the Kingdom of God must be transformed into a life style the world can see and comprehend. (See Rev. 5:9-10; 11:15 and 20:4). Heaven is not a place, but a realm of the Spirit and a state of being. God dwells in heaven and if you have been born again (from above), God is in you, therefore heaven is within you. We are the temple of the living God. (1 Cor. 3:16-17)

The born again Christians living here on earth today make up the body of our Lord Jesus Christ. He is the head over the sons of God (both male and female), the leadership company, who in turn rule the remainder of the biblical Christians. These same sons extend their rule to the realm of outer darkness, those void of spiritual understanding. (1 Cor. 6:19; 11:3; 12:27; Eph. 1:22-23; 5:23) Isaiah 9:6 states that the government (of the Kingdom) shall be upon His (Christ's) shoulders. His shoulders are the sons of God.

Remember, "Thy kingdom come, thy will be done **in earth** as it is in heaven." (Matt. 6:10) It is clear from Scripture that God is more interested in getting heaven (or the realm of the spirit) into us or operating in us than getting us into heaven. How then is the Kingdom expressed in the earth today? By the (true) church.

What is the Church? In the Old Testament, the Kingdom of God was to be expressed through natural Israel. In the time of the New Testament however, the Kingdom of God is expressed through spiritual Israel, which is the Church. The Church is Abraham's seed (Gal. 3:28-29); a holy nation (1 Pet. 2:9-10.); His body (Eph. 1:22-23), and the temple where God dwells (1 Cor 3:16-17). The Church is the Ecclesia, or the "called out" (Eph. 1:22, Concordant Literal N.T.), those born anew by the Spirit of Jesus Christ. The word "Kingdom" speaks of God's purpose or the extension of His rule and reign. The term "church," on the other hand, speaks of the present instrument whereby that purpose is realized.

The Kingdom of God manifests itself in the earth, not in plants, animals, inanimate objects, or the unsaved, but in a people called "**the Church.**" This is a present reality, a phase of the Kingdom which began on the day of Pentecost.

The Kingdom of God on earth is the manifestation of the rule and will of God through His sons in earth, as it is now in heaven. Whereas the Kingdom of God in heaven (the spiritual realm) is a fact, the Kingdom of

God in the earth is a progressive development. It is progressive because it depends upon an increasing spiritual awareness of each member of the Kingdom concerning the laws of the Kingdom and how they function and operate in the everyday lives of the people of the Kingdom.

Where is the Kingdom? Let us read from *The Prophetic Community* by Earl Paulk, p 17, "The Kingdom of God is in the heart. It is your heart God is after. That is the place where He does His work. Once you understand that the Kingdom is in your heart, and you follow its laws as a part of your daily life, then the Kingdom exists wherever you are."

The Manifestation of the Sons of God

Once we were servants of sin (Rom. 6:20), even enemies of God, but once we became born anew or born from above, we became servants of God (Rom. 6:22). Now God longs for us to grow or change from that servant realm to a son realm. We read in Phileman 16 that when Onenesimus returns, he returns not as a servant but as a beloved brother. Jesus came to redeem us and bring us into full sonship. "Therefore you are no longer a slave (bond servant) but a son, and if a son, then [it follows that you are] an heir by the aid of God, *through Christ*." (Gal. 4:7 AMP) Galatians 4:5 (NAS) explains that "we might receive the adoption as sons."

Who is a son of God? Most importantly, he is one led by the Spirit of God (Rom. 8:14). This verse states "As many as are led by the Spirit of God, they are the sons of God." The term "as many" indicates that not all are led by the (Holy) Spirit. Why are some led and some not? I believe it is because some people will never advance far enough in the Kingdom to learn how to be led by the Spirit. Such people don't practice a regular prayer life or read and study their Bible regularly, fail to obey the truth, or refuse to digest any Scripture beyond the milk stage. Furthermore, with the (Holy) Spirit they do have, they don't allow Him to take control over their flesh.

In Romans 8:19 we read, "For the earnest expectation of the creature waiteth for the manifestation of the sons of God." Another way of saying it may be: "...waiting for the manifestation of God through the sons." God expressed Himself in the earth in the form of a man, Jesus Christ. God's desire now is to express Himself, His character, His nature and His attributes to all mankind via the sons of God to the world.

"And all of us, as with unveiled face, [because we] continued to behold [in the Word of God] as in a mirror the glory of the Lord, are constantly being transfigured into His *very own* image in ever increasing splendor *and* from one degree of glory to another, [for this comes] from the Lord [Who is] the Spirit" (2 Cor. 3:18 AMP.). This verse tells us that man is yet to come fully into the image of God, but that he is progressing toward that goal. It's through the leadership and ministry of the sons of God that man advances toward that image of God. Without that leadership, man, even the Christian, gropes in the darkness of religion.

1 Corinthians 15:45, the Amplified Bible states: "Thus it is written, The first Adam became a living being—an individual personality; the last Adam (Christ) became a **life giving spirit** —restoring the dead to life." Verse 49 (AMP) goes on to say, "And just as we have borne the image of the [man] of dust, so shall we *and* so let us bear the image of the [**Man**] of heaven." That growth process, into the image of Christ, continues until we become, as Christ, totally life giving. God now longs for a son (a many membered son) in His image to perpetuate His seed, His nature, and His ministry in the earth, through our physical bodies.

God first demonstrated through the Person of Jesus Christ of Nazareth that His (God's) image could be manifested in human form in a finite body in the midst of the environment and culture of the earth, in the heart of the everyday life of man, reaching down to the depths of their sin and into the depths of their hurts. God demonstrated that through Jesus He could touch mankind who was sick in spirit, soul and body. In this role, as Jesus walked the earth, He was 100 % God and 100 % man (Isa. 9:6; John 1:1-2; 14:7-10; Phil. 2:5-9).

Beginning on the day of Pentecost, Jesus Christ, possessing the attributes and the very life of God, dwelt **within** certain men and began to manifest Himself in and through these men (the first 120), allowing that new divine nature to come forth. By this manner God established the throne of David in the earth. This was the beginning of the manifestation of the Kingdom of God in the earth! "Who (Jesus Christ) is the image of the invisible God, the firstborn of every creature." (Col. 1:15) Man receives this new nature via the rebirth from above (John. 3:3). He is a new creature in Christ Jesus (2 Cor. 5:17), but not yet a son.

As we put on the Lord Jesus Christ, we aren't speaking of just the future, but **now.** God is NOW forming a people into the image and likeness of His Son, Jesus Christ, a people who speak life and who walk out and live the life of which they speak. We change into His image by a process. (See 2 Cor. 3:18 above). "At that day ye shall know that I am in my Father, and ye in me, and I in you." (John 14:20) Yes, we will come to totally know this truth! See also John 17:23; Ephesians 3:17-19 and Galatians. 1:24 which bear witness to the indwelling Christ. Christ in you, the hope of glory (Col. 1:27). Pray for God to reveal this truth to you if you don't already see it.

Concerning another aspect of our identity, let me quote from *For God's Sake, Grow Up* by David Ravenhill (p 51): "Moses crying out to God, '...so that we, I and Thy people, may be distinguished from all the other people who are upon the face of the earth' (Ex. 33:15-16). It's not our doctrine or creed, our law or lifestyle that makes us different. The one and only thing that makes you and me distinct is His presence. A singleness of desire after God is the hallmark of the true child of God."

If we have been born from above, then we recognize the Spirit of Jesus Christ within us (2 Cor. 6:16). He dwells in the hearts of believers (Eph. 3:17). We are new creatures in Christ Jesus, for our old adamic man has been crucified. Jesus, the King of the Kingdom, manifests Himself in a people, the sonship company, right now (2 Pet. 1:4)! If we continue to postpone His appearing into the future, then we have missed it.

No one can take a short cut to God. All must pass by the brazen altar in the outer court (salvation) and through the Holy Place (baptism of the Holy Spirit) to reach the Most Holy Place where man can dwell in the presence of God. In reality, the Most Holy Place is within you, for that is where God dwells—in His throne (John 17:21, 23; Col. 1:27; Rev. 3:21). We speak of an experience here and now on this earth.

Jesus as King

Jesus as King reigns in peace in the kingdom; He reigns in righteousness, righteousness not established by external laws or regulations but through the hearts of people. He came not to condemn the world but to save it. (John 3:17)

"Now he who keeps His commandments abides in Him, and He in him. And by this we know that He abides in us, by the Spirit whom He has given us." (1 John 3:24 NKJV) Later in the earthly ministry of Jesus, His disciples believed that He was the Son of God. "He (Jesus) saith unto them, But who say ye that I am? and Simon Peter answered and said, Thou art the Christ, the Son of the living God." (Matt. 16:16)

In Matthew 27:11 we read, "And Jesus stood before the governor: and the governor asked him, saying, Art thou the King of the Jews? And Jesus said unto him, Thou sayest." The NKJV reads, "...It is as you say" with the words "It is as" in italics, indicating it isn't in the original. So the original simply says, "you say". Jesus did not deny He was the king of the Jews nor did He confirm it. "He came unto his own (the Jews) and his own received him not.". (John 1:11) He came to the Jews as a Savior, not as king.

Jesus emphasized that his Kingdom was not an earthly kingdom. "Jesus answered (Pilate), My Kingdom (kingship, royal power) belongs not to this world. If My kingdom were of the world, My followers would have been fighting to keep Me from being handed over to the Jews. But as it is, My kingdom is not from [this world]—has no such origin or source." (John. 18:36 AMP) The NAS version states it this way, "...My kingdom is not of this realm." In essence, He was saying: "The Kingdom of God is not of this kosmos or orderly arrangement, not a part of the present political, social, economic, or religious systems."

Continuing in verse 37, "Pilate therefore said unto him, Art thou a king then? Jesus answered, Thou sayest that I am a king. To this end was I born, and for this cause came I into the world, that I should bear witness unto the truth. Every one that is of the truth heareth my voice." Why was Jesus born or why did He come into the world? That He should bear witness to the truth. Not once in scripture does Jesus confess that He was a king over any earthly group of people. He called Himself the "Son of Man," not a "king".

Paul wrote, "...the carnal mind is enmity against God: for it is not subject to the law of God, neither indeed can be" (Rom. 8:7). The carnal mind concerns itself only in the physical realm or the flesh. Therefore the carnal mind was never designed to reign (as king), either in the world or in our own life. It brings to ruin every kingdom it possesses, because it is concerned with self. It eventually becomes corrupted because it makes self the center rather than God. It has manifested itself in men like Pharaoh and Herod who tried to destroy those that would oppose them. In the history of man and even today, it has sought and now seeks to destroy all that is godly. But Jesus Christ is the one who reigns as King in the Kingdom of God.

Establishment of the Kingdom

When was the kingdom of God established? Or are we waiting until some distant future for its establishment? Let us turn to the book of Daniel to see the establishment of this Kingdom of God. "And in the days of these kings shall the God of heaven set up a kingdom, which shall never be destroyed: and the kingdom shall not be left to other people, but it shall break in pieces and consume all these kingdoms, and it shall stand for ever." (Dan. 2:44) The phrase "days of these kings" shows us the establishment of the Kingdom. It was when those kings reigned.

"And there was given him dominion, and glory, and a kingdom, that all people, nations, and languages, should serve him: his dominion is an ever-lasting dominion, which shall not pass away, and his kingdom that which shall not be destroyed." (Dan. 7:14) Verse 18 states, "But the saints of the most High shall take the kingdom, and possess the kingdom for ever, even for ever and ever." This truth represents the eternal plan or purpose of God, the establishment of the eternal Kingdom.

Daniel 7:27 points to the sons of God who reign in the Kingdom: "And the kingdom and dominion, and the greatness of the kingdom under the whole heaven, shall be given to the people of the saints of the most High, whose kingdom is an everlasting kingdom, and all dominions shall serve and obey him."

In the book of Daniel, chapter 3, we see an important aspect of the operation of the Kingdom where the three Hebrew children refused to bow to the image of the earthly king. This account illustrates how believers should act in the Kingdom today. The children of the Kingdom today should not bow, that is, show allegiance to earthly systems, but to the one and only God. As children of the Kingdom, we should not bow to the gods of self, sports, TV, secular humanism or the philosophies and systems of men. What a world this would be if believers did not bow to these gods

God's primary objective in sending His Son was not to save us but to establish His Kingdom. Jesus Christ saved us, not just to be saved but so that He would plant His seed within us to give us new life. Throughout the gospels, Jesus taught the Kingdom with word pictures, that is, parables that the ordinary person could understand. He further demonstrated that the Kingdom is not just an idea, an abstract thought or figure of speech nor a futuristic Disney World, but a present reality. After Pentecost the Kingdom became a reality in the hearts of believers. When people think they can postpone the Kingdom to some future time, then they feel they don't have to deal with their problems now.

Isaiah had prophesied that in a time of restoration God would visit His people and that a messenger would precede Him (Isa. 40:3). Isaiah prophesied also concerning the coming Messiah and His Kingdom, "For he shall grow up before him as a tender plant, and as a root out of a dry ground: he hath no form nor comeliness; and when we shall see him, there is no beauty that we should desire him." (Isa. 53:2)

John the Baptist was that messenger, and the Lord coming to His temple was the Holy Spirit. Jesus went into the synagogue and read from Isaiah (Luke 4:16-21) and declared, "This day is this scripture fulfilled in your ears."

How does Jesus rule over His Kingdom? We must first state that He does not rule by force. You remember when Peter smote off the servant's ear with his sword. (John 18:10) Jesus rebuked him and told him to put his sword back in the sheath. We can view this literally or spiritually. The sword represents force. Jesus administers in the Kingdom, not by military, political or even economic force, but by the cross. We know the sword represents the Word of God or the Bible (Heb. 4:12). The saints of the Kingdom do not rule by hitting people over the head with the Bible. That is, they don't quote Scripture to people in a spirit of condemnation. We sometimes need to keep our sword in its sheath. In other words, we may need to lay or Bible down and just listen to someone, child or adult alike. The cross, not the sword, wins people's hearts for the Lord. Jesus, as our example, chose to walk the way of the cross and obey His Father.

The further establishment of the Kingdom of God doesn't come through political or military power or action, not by marches on Washington. The rulership order of the Kingdom of God won't possess or conquer the world by carnal means for that would destroy, not build, men's lives. God doesn't force a person to obey His laws, yet that's how many perceive the rule of the Kingdom. They believe that some day, Jesus Christ will come in person and with His vast armies will force all people to obey His laws to the letter or be thrown in jail.

God's laws, founded on love, operate today in the hearts of men and women. Jesus is the light. And there was light and "In Him was life, and the life was the light of men." (John 1:4) This life we speak of is resurrection life, the greatest power in the universe. The power of that light is love. Such a power does not operate by force but by life giving, transforming power, changing the very lives of men and women and is the power of the Kingdom of God. The Kingdom of God is within, for life is within.

Love changes the nature of people and wins allegiance from the heart. Jesus demonstrated this love of the Father in His three and one half years on the earth. Now, through His saints, He continues via the indwelling Christ, to demonstrate that same love to each other and to the world.

In the wilderness temptation, Jesus rejected the temptation to be leader of the kingdoms of the world. He knew that the rule of the Kingdom of God was something higher than mere natural power. Jesus also made it clear in His teachings that the rule of the Kingdom was intended for all men and not for just for the "chosen people" (Matt. 8:11).

Jesus rejected the temptation to turn the stones into bread, to become the economic leader who would gratify the materialistic longing of his people. He rejected the temptation to throw Himself down, symbolizing miracles. The most important meaning of His messianic ministry was not in the role of a worldly hero but in the role of a suffering servant.

Jesus realized that He had to suffer and die in order to usher in the Kingdom. But only through His death and resurrection could the present corruption of the Levitical priesthood by its leaders be overcome and the Kingdom of God come into its power to free mankind from all oppression.

In his earthly ministry, Jesus emphasized the religious aspects of the rule in the Kingdom. That God would rule over the hearts of men was of utmost importance. In that day man's problem was not the tyranny of Rome or physical hunger but separation from God. Today mankind faces the same problem. Their problem is not with government forces, powers of the world, economic strife or hunger but separation from God. In His earthly ministry, Jesus taught little about political freedom or freedom from hunger but about reconciliation with God and about life in the Kingdom.

All of His parables and sayings explain various aspects of God's purpose and of man's relationship to God and to his fellow-men in the Kingdom of

God. Christ first however, desires to establish His Kingdom *in us* before He can establish His Kingdom *through us*.

Jesus demonstrated to us in His life as God on the earth in the form of a servant in the likeness of man (Phil. 2:7) that He intends to save mankind within our environment in the earth and within our daily lives, not apart from it. He likewise not only identified Himself with man but also brought man to God.

The people in the day of Jesus expected a Messiah to rule by force. They, and even His disciples had ignored or not understood the teaching of Jesus on how God, in the Kingdom would rule through the hearts of men.— aspects of God's love and man's joyful obedience. When a person truly loves God, is born anew, he obeys God, not out of a sense of duty but with joy and love in his heart. This is a true mark of a child of the Kingdom.

How is the Kingdom of God established? Spiritual power, a power that transforms men's lives from the inside out, and men who become new creatures in Christ Jesus establish it. Political action will not bring about the Kingdom of God. The Kingdom of God is righteousness, peace and joy in the Holy Ghost. We certainly need better laws and more efficient government but when these governments, corporations, businesses, schools and other institutions change because the people within them change by the regeneration of the Holy Spirit, then we have the Kingdom of God. As the Kingdom progresses, some of these systems will be radically changed while some will be eliminated. ."...The kingdoms of this world are become the kingdoms of our Lord, and of his Christ;..." (Rev. 11:15)

Our choices in our outer world should serve to express the reality of what we really are in our inner world, that is, our real self. When we choose a job, we don't choose on the basis of its value to the outer world, but we choose that which will express our inner man. That is where we find peace, joy and righteousness. That is where the Kingdom of God is and where true life is, where reality is and where heaven is. The only real quality in life is the inward man which is Christ.

The deplorable condition of our society today will not improve by passing more laws or by stricter law enforcement, but by people who live out the life of Christ under the power and direction of the Holy Spirit.

After the day of Pentecost, we find the 12 disciples (if we include Matthias), and not long after, the Apostle Paul, through the power of the Holy Spirit and the Word of God, turned the world upside down and brought new light to a world groping in darkness.

The Kingdom of God within you

Jesus declared, "The Kingdom of God is within you." It's within men that changes are made. Our problems of crime, sickness and death are but symptoms of the internal sin of man. When man is born anew or from above, he receives a new nature, the nature of God, which is love, peace and joy- wherein, the power of the Kingdom of God. Our old Adamic man was crucified on the cross. The Kingdom of God is now brought to reality through the inworking of God in the new creation man. The seed of Christ in each of the born again persons is an incorruptible seed, identical to the Christ seed.

The purpose of the new birth is to give us the life of God, which is the life of the Kingdom of God. As God perfects and raises up this life in us, the Kingdom of God is established within us by life and as life. As Jesus proclaimed so well, that every branch that bears fruit, God purges it so that it may bring forth more fruit. Just as pruning grapes brings forth fuller and richer grapevines, so such pruning concentrates the life of Christ within us. The fruit we bear is not saving souls, but the manifestation of the nature and character of the Christ within us, the same character as the parent Seed that was planted in us, for seeds produce according to their own kind (John 15:1-2; Gen. 1:25).

An interesting aspect of the Kingdom of God appears in Luke 23:40-43 concerning the conversation of one of the malefactors on the cross (v. 39). "But the other answering rebuked him, saying, Dost not thou fear God, seeing thou art in the same condemnation? (41) And we indeed justly; for we receive the due reward of our deeds: but this man hath done nothing amiss. (42) And he said unto Jesus, Lord, remember me when thou comest into thy kingdom. (43) And Jesus said unto him, Verily I say unto thee, To day shalt thou be with me in paradise."

The word "paradise" means a park, and is not heaven but more of a condition than a geographical place; that is, it is a place of rest. The Kingdom is a place of rest in God, here and now in this life.

The word "malefactor" means a wrong doer (Strong's #2557), generally a political troublemaker, one who rebels or insurrects, one who looked for the overthrow of the Roman Government. The malefactor sensed something about Jesus coming into or establishing His Kingdom. He perceived Jesus was coming into a different type of Kingdom, an entirely different realm than the one present under Roman rule or the rule of Judaism or even the rule of the natural man. Notice He emphasized Your (NKJV) Kingdom. He sensed that Jesus would have authority or rule as King in that Kingdom. He also sensed that the true life of Jesus would not end there on the cross but that now Jesus would enter into a new life, a new realm, or a new dimension, and even thought that he could enter into that same Kingdom.

The word "remember"- (v 42) from Strong's #3415 means the idea of fixture in the mind, a mental grasp, to bear in mind i.e. to recollect, by impl. to reward or punish. The malefactor asked Jesus not just to remember him by a mere thought. Rather he spoke from a repentant heart. Jesus therefore recognized his sincerity and repentant heart and rewarded him.

CHAPTER 2

▼

WHEN IS THE KINGDOM OF GOD MANIFESTED?

The Kingdom of Heaven at Hand

The prophets of the Old Testament proclaimed that God's eternal rule would be manifested on the earth through the reign of the coming Messiah. (Isa. 9:6-7; Mic. 5:2). "In that day will I raise up the tabernacle of David that is fallen..." (Amos 9:11). We are that tabernacle of David. John the Baptist declared the same literal Kingdom on the earth, as did the prophets.

Moving on now to the New Testament, John the Baptist was the forerunner of the earthly ministry of Jesus as he proclaimed the Kingdom. "In those days John the Baptist came preaching in the wilderness of Judea, and saying, 'Repent, for the kingdom of heaven is at hand!' For this is he who was spoken of by the prophet Isaiah, saying: 'The voice of one crying in

the wilderness: 'Prepare the way of the LORD; Make His paths straight.'"
(Matt. 3:1-3 NKJV; Isa. 40:3).

The word **"repent"** here means to change your way of thinking or to
turn around and go the other way. John was talking not only to the multitude, but also to the Pharisees, the religious leaders of the day. The self
righteous Pharisees and Sadducees thought that because they were a natural descendant of Abraham, they were already members of the Kingdom of
God. But unfortunately, they rejected the message John proclaimed.
Accordingly, he called them a brood of vipers (v. 7).

By the Old Testament law, a viper was not only unclean but would
defile anything it contacted. In effect, John accused them of not only
being unclean but that they defiled the people they contacted and taught.

Their main false teaching claimed that a natural descendant of
Abraham automatically entered the Kingdom of God. "But when he
(John) saw many of the Pharisees and Sadducees come to his baptism, he
said unto them, O generation of vipers, who hath warned you to flee from
the wrath to come? Bring forth therefore fruits meet for repentance: And
think not to say within yourselves, We have Abraham to our father: for I
say unto you, that God is able of these stones to raise up children unto
Abraham." (Matt. 3:7-8)

Think of introducing a candidate for president of the United States on
such a negative note. **"Repent!"** Or think of introducing the new president of a large corporation, a man from outside the company to the board
of directors. Would we ever find such a critical approach? Yet, that is the
approach John the Baptist used.

What did John mean, "The kingdom of heaven is at hand?" The Greek
word for "at hand" means "near." "Near" can refer to geography or to
time. As to geography, Jesus, the central point of the Kingdom, was in
their midst. As to time, Jesus would begin preaching and demonstrating
the principles of the Kingdom. "At hand" also means that the kingdom
was now within reach of all mankind, an opportunity for all nations, races
and tongues. Later Paul declared, "There is neither Jew nor Greek, there is

neither slave nor free, there is neither male nor female; for you are all one in Christ Jesus." (Gal. 3:28)

Jesus, the central figure of the kingdom, came from Galilee to Jordan to be baptized by John. "I indeed baptize you with water unto repentance, but He who is coming after me is mightier than I, whose sandals I am not worthy to carry. He will baptize you with the Holy Spirit and fire." (Matt. 3:11).

Until John the Baptist, Israel had waited 430 years since the time of the prophet Malachi to hear from God (Mal. 3:1). They had even waited hundreds of years since hearing the prophecies in the Old Testament, which pointed to the coming Messiah, and His Kingdom. Now they were told that the long awaited and expected Messiah and His Kingdom were near.

He was at hand—was within reach of not only the people of Israel but to all mankind. They wouldn't have to wait 2-3,000 years, nor would they have to wait until they died and went to the other side (however you might express it). Near—the Kingdom of God in the earth was on hand, to effect their everyday lives. They wouldn't have to wait for another dimension, for in three and a half years Jesus Christ would return via the Holy Spirit to dwell in the hearts of men.

• God had now introduced a personalized Kingdom, ruled by a king who would not just talk and communicate with leaders as God had done with Abraham and Moses and the prophets of the Old Testament, but He would talk and relate to each and every man, woman and child on a continual basis. He would be as close as their breath, for He would be in them.

John the Baptist could have been a temple priest, for his father was a Levitical priest (Luke 1:5), however he chose instead to begin his preaching in the wilderness, outside the prevailing religious system. He wore camel's hair and ate locusts and honey—a further departure from the traditional. Clothing speaks of spiritual covering. For John, his covering was not of the Levitical priesthood, but of the Melchisedec order. The locusts and honey, natural food, symbolized spiritual food, direct from God rather than from man.

Jesus similarly wasn't born in a palace, nor was He from the tribe of Levi but of Judah. Neither was He raised in a household of high rank in the prevailing religious system. Here, we see a sharp departure from the religious system of the time. So it has been over the centuries. Every major move of God began outside the prevailing religious system. We find Martin Luther and his clinging to the Scriptures, "The just shall live by faith," John Wesley and Methodism, the Pentecostal movement of the early 1900's, the Latter Rain movement of 1948, and the sonship teaching of Bill Britton, begun in the early sixties, all started primarily outside the prevailing religious systems.

John spoke to those outside the religious system as well as the religious leaders of the day. The common people asked "What shall we do then?" (Luke. 3:10). John demanded the same fruit of real repentance from these people as he had from the Pharisees. One evidence of this repentance was a concern for the poor. He taught the tax gatherers to refrain from collecting excess tax (v. 13), which they had put in their own pockets. He further taught that soldiers should prove their repentance by not misusing their authority (v. 14). He instructed them, "Be content with your wages."

John indicated to those he taught that when a person submitted to water baptism, the external sign, that they truly accepted His teaching or message. But he also declared that there was one coming who would baptize them with the Holy Spirit, **an internal baptism.** "John answered, saying unto them all, I indeed baptize you with water; but one mightier than I cometh, the latchet of whose shoes I am not worthy to unloose: he shall baptize you with the Holy Ghost and with fire: Whose fan is in his hand, and he will thoroughly purge his floor, and will gather the wheat into his garner; but the chaff he will burn with fire unquenchable." (Luke 3:16-17) A fan is a five-pronged fork, symbolic of the Word of God in the five-fold ministry.

Contrasted with the external sign, neither man nor the religious systems of men could duplicate the internal sign. Yet, such a sign would identify the true Messiah. (v 16). He would also baptize you with fire. Fire is associated with judgment. But the fire of judgment isn't a literal fire but an internal work of the Holy Spirit who burns up all the hay, wood, stubble, and chaff in our life. These are the things and thoughts that are without life, those that are not of God (1 Cor. 3:13-15).

In Bible numerology, two is the number of witness. Throughout the Bible, God both instructs and demonstrates this principle. Jesus declared in Matthew 18:16, "...That in the mouth of two or three witnesses every word may be established." (See also John 8:17-18; Deut. 19:15; Rom 3:21; John 5:31-37).

At the time that John baptized Jesus, God manifested two witnesses that Jesus was exactly who John had proclaimed Him to be—the awaited Messiah, the Saviour of the world, the King of the Kingdom. These two witnesses were the *sight* and the *sound*.

The Holy Spirit descending on Him in bodily form like a dove (Luke 3:22) emerged as the sight witness. As an audible sign, they heard a voice from heaven, the sound and second witness. "And lo a voice from heaven, saying, This is my beloved Son, in whom I am well pleased." (Matt. 3:17).

Where did that voice come from? It didn't just come out of the sky or out of the air. Audible voices come from people. If it came from heaven, as the scripture states, then it had to come from the heavenly or spiritual realm, that is, a person filled with the spirit of God. Who was present that would qualify? Besides Jesus, it could be none other than John the Baptist. He was filled with the Holy Spirit from his mother's womb (Luke 1:15). And we know that he grew and waxed strong in spirit (Luke 1:80). I believe it was John who spoke that prophetic word.

Jesus voiced words similar to that of John when He began to preach. "Now after John was put in prison, Jesus came to Galilee, preaching the gospel of the Kingdom of God, and saying, "The time is fulfilled, and the kingdom of God is at hand. **Repent,** and believe in the gospel." (Mark 1:14-15). In the Old Testament, God spoke from the mountain and warned the common people, "Keep away" (Exod. 19:12). In contrast, the message of the New Testament invites all to come—all races, creeds, nationalities and tongues.

The Kingdom was at hand. Jesus began His earthly ministry and not only taught the principles of the Kingdom but also put them into practice and demonstrated how to live in the Kingdom. The power necessary, however, for man to enter, live, grow and function actively in the Kingdom, would not come until the day of Pentecost, when the Holy Spirit would come to live and abide in certain people. The Holy Spirit would then bring to the disciples' remembrance all that Jesus had taught (John 14:26). The Holy Spirit does the same today for born again, Spirit-filled believers. That is, He reveals the meaning of the Scriptures, and brings them back to our remembrance to help us in our time of need, whether that need is to seek deeper truths or to guide us in our Christian walk. When Peter confessed to Jesus that He was the Christ, Jesus told him "...for flesh and blood has not revealed this to you, but My Father who is in heaven" (Matt. 16:17 NKJV). Jesus also declared, "...on this rock [petr *a*, feminine, a huge rock like Gibraltar] I will build My church. (Matt. 16:18 AMP). That rock is revelation knowledge.

Through the power of the Holy Spirit (Acts 1:8) a believer can really live and wholly participate in the Kingdom of God. Profession by faith for salvation alone isn't sufficient evidence or knowledge to operate in the Kingdom. The gospel of salvation and the gospel of the Kingdom are two entirely different things. "For the kingdom of God is not in word, but in power." (1 Cor. 4:20) When we are saved however, and filled with the Holy Spirit, we **should** begin to demonstrate the power of that Kingdom of God in our daily lives.

A newborn baby becomes a member of a family and a citizen of the country in which it is born, but until it grows and matures, that child comprehends nothing about what's going on in the country or even its own family. So too, a newly born again (anew) person has salvation of his spirit but doesn't have a clue as to what's going on in the Kingdom. He has to grow into that knowledge.

The Kingdom of God has now come, through the leadership company of the sons of God, to the ordinary man—to guide, to direct, to comfort and even to correct him in his everyday life. He now has Jesus Christ who will forgive his or her sins, a Jesus they can talk to, not through a priest, but one on one. Man no longer depends on animal sacrifices, for Jesus was the perfect and final sacrifice. Man can become the true seed of Abraham by faith. (Rom. 2:28-29; 4:16; Heb. 9:11-14)

Growth of the Kingdom

The Kingdom is progressive. It has been established, it is now being developed and it will be continue to grow in the future. This growth of the Kingdom is a progressive revelation and fulfillment of God's plan and purpose in the earth. The disciples did not envision Jesus appearing as king years or centuries later but He was King to them then and He is King now. The disciples knew Jesus Christ was already coroneted by the Father in heaven. He was not waiting 2,000 years to be crowned. "Therefore let all the house of Israel know assuredly, that God hath made that same Jesus, whom ye have crucified, both Lord and Christ." (Acts 2:36)

"But we see Jesus, who was made a little lower (Greek word meaning to lessen, in rank or influence) than the angels (Gr: Elohim or Most High God) for the suffering of death, crowned with glory and honour; that he by the grace of God should taste death for every man." (Heb. 2:9)

Paul declared in Colossians 1:12-13, "Giving thanks unto the Father, which hath made us meet to be partakers of the inheritance of the saints in light: Who hath delivered us from the power of darkness, and hath translated us into the kingdom of his dear Son:" This is past tense. We are already translated; we are in the Kingdom now, walking around in shoe leather in our present body. Jesus said, "But I tell you of a truth, there be some standing here, which shall not taste of death, till they see the Kingdom of God" (Luke 9:27). On the day of Pentecost, some of those people who heard the Lord speak those words would certainly see some of the manifestation of the Kingdom.

God the Father, not man, builds the Kingdom. Jesus instructed men how to accept, enter and live in the Kingdom, but never to create or build it. If this is true, then what can man do in regard to the Kingdom? "But seek ye first the kingdom of God, and his righteousness; and all these things shall be added unto you." (Matt. 6:33) "To seek first" means to make the Kingdom our number one priority.

How do we, as believers, do that? We walk in the Kingdom principles set out in the Scriptures, or in other words, we obey the Scriptures. For starters, we study the Sermon on the Mount (Matthew, chapters 5—7). We also submit to the rule of the King, the Lord Jesus Christ and to His leadership order (the sons of God) in all aspects of our lives.

As for man, the manifestation of the Kingdom of God **within** man began on the day of Pentecost. Jesus said, "If I go away, I will come again" and this He did on the day of Pentecost. This time however, He did not come in human form but in the essence of His being which is spirit. He came not to simply be with us but now to dwell within us (John 14:7). This was the indwelling Christ. This is God who is Spirit. Paul declared "If we are joined unto the Lord we are one spirit. (1 Cor. 6:17). We read of this in Acts, "When the Day of Pentecost had fully come, they were all with one accord in one place....And they were all filled with the Holy Spirit and began to speak with other tongues, as the Spirit gave them utterance." (Acts 2:1-4 NKJV)

Jesus had foretold to His disciples this presence of the Holy Spirit within them. (John 16:7) The Lord also told His disciples: "And I will pray the Father, and he shall give you another Comforter, that he may abide with you for ever; Even the Spirit of truth; whom the world cannot receive, because it seeth him not, neither knoweth him: but ye know him; for he dwelleth with you, and **shall be in you.**" (John 14:16-17)

The parable of the mustard seed illustrates how the Kingdom of God would start small and appear insignificant, but would grow into a kingdom that would shelter (as this herb shelters the birds) all of God's people (Mark 4:30-32). The expanse and rule of the Kingdom grows, from this likeness of the mustard seed, to Jesus as the Son of God, possessing all power (rule and authority), not just in the earth (earthly realm) but likewise in the heavens (heavenly or spiritual realm).

In the Jewish culture of that day, they held strict rules, even about planting a garden, such as forbidding the mixing of certain plants in the same garden. A mustard seed planted in a garden of vegetables would soon spread to take over the whole garden. Likewise the Kingdom of God will grow to take over or greatly influence our everyday lives. Jesus dispels any thought of the hearers expecting the mustard to grow to the height of the majestic cedars of Lebanon, which by the way, matures very slowly. The Kingdom of God is here and now in our every day lives. We don't have to wait for some future spectacular event to see or enter the kingdom. Nor do we have to "die and go to heaven" as some imagine.

The greatest accomplishments of the Kingdom are the changes in our attitudes, our thought life, and the growth of the inner man, largely unseen by the natural eye, in secret as it were. Many look for the Kingdom to fully manifest on a given day of the calendar, taking over all the societies and people of the earth. If we are looking first for rapid expansion of the external, the social movements, a particular denomination or nation, we have missed it.

"And Jesus came and spake unto them, saying, All power is given unto me in heaven and in earth." (Matt. 28:18) However, Jesus Christ transfers that same power to the leadership company or the sons of God (John 17). We look to Jesus' prayer in John 17:2 where He says, "As thou hast given him power over all flesh, that he should give eternal life to as many as thou hast given him."

Now verse 3, "And this is life eternal, that they (the leadership company) might know thee the only true God,..." Verse 6, "I have manifested thy name unto the men (the leadership company) which thou gavest me out of the world: thine they were, and thou gavest them me; and they have kept thy word." Verse 8 goes on to say, "For I have given unto them (the leadership company) the words which thou gavest me; and they have received them,…" Verse 10, "…and I am glorified in them (the leadership company). Now verse 18, "As thou hast sent me into the world, even so have I also sent them (the leadership company) into the world.". (Parentheses this author).

In other words, to the leadership company, God has granted eternal life, that they might know God; Jesus has manifested the name or nature of God to them; He has given them the words of the Father and He is glorified in them and has sent them into the world.

The Lord Jesus has given His authority to the five fold ministry or the leadership (sonship) company to rule and reign in the Kingdom of God (Eph. 4:8-13). What about the subjects that these leaders rule over? Subjects of the Kingdom dwell in differing degrees of darkness or light. We find that those in outer darkness (void of any spiritual understanding) dwell in varying stages of that darkness. Those in the 30-fold realm (who have some light) dwell all the way from one to 30 in their walk in the kingdom. When a person is just saved, they dwell at "one" with just a flicker of spiritual light. Then those in the 60-fold realm may operate anywhere from 31 to 60. See the chapter 4 on the Three Experiences of the Believer for further details.

A symbol of the growth of the Kingdom emerges from Mark 4:26-28, "And he said, So is the kingdom of God, as if a man should cast seed into the ground; And should sleep, and rise night and day, and the seed should spring and grow up, he knoweth not how. For the earth bringeth forth fruit of herself; first the blade, then the ear, after that the full corn in the ear."

Spiritual growth in the Kingdom doesn't come about because man gets more involved in politics or social programs, but grows by the power of Holy Spirit working within the believers. Such growth is a sovereign work of God. You plant a kernel of beans in the ground. You can water it and allow the sun to shine on it, but it still grows by the power of God. "I have planted, Apollos watered; but God gave the increase." (1 Cor. 3:6)

Furthermore, you can't easily measure growth within a plant. Neither can you see nor measure spiritual growth within an individual member of the Kingdom. Spiritual growth of individuals in the Kingdom is part of the plan of God (Heb. 6:1; 1 Pet. 2:2; 2 Pet. 3:18). We realize however, that some individuals grow faster than others do. We should add that it is imperative that we, as individuals, should determine to grow spiritually. When a plant stops growing, it starts to die. People in the kingdom likewise die spiritually when they stop to grow.

The Church and the Kingdom

We stated in the first chapter that the Church is the vehicle by which the Kingdom of God is expressed in the earth. By the "church" we mean the called out ones, a holy nation, or Abraham's seed. One of the keys to living in the Kingdom of God however, is a strong local church, made up of members of the Church universal. Such a church preaches the uncompromising Word of God. The members possess strong prayer lives, tithe regularly and freely give offerings. They demonstrate dependability and commitment to the body of Christ and to the local assembly. The members are active in mission and evangelistic programs as well as in fellowship with other local churches. These local churches either have or are working toward a five-fold ministry. The members live as overcomers in the Kingdom. In whatever spiritual growth the members of the local church dwell, they seek to move higher in the Lord. We must emphasize that the Holy Spirit rather than the letter of the law will lead these activities.

The local church is the family of God. In the active local church, members care and intercede for one another on a personal daily basis, encourage and help others in their spiritual walk. They relate like brothers and sisters for they are. Local church members get more satisfaction in fellowshipping with their brothers and sisters in the Lord than they get in shopping, sports or any other worldly activity. The pastors or shepherds of the strong local churches know their sheep by name (nature), and are willing to lay down their life for them. A strong local church disciples their new converts as well as their children and youth. Every day Jesus took His disciples apart and discipled them. The members of a strong local church attend services regularly and display loyalty to the leadership and other members of the assembly. They lay their critical or contentious spirit at the cross and cast aside all semblance of bickering and murmuring.

"Of the increase of his government and peace there shall be no end,..." (Isa. 9:7) That government of the Kingdom, with the sons of God in a leadership role, shall have no end. Rank in the kingdom shall continue for ages and ages to come. Leaders with subjects under them will always continue to exist in the Kingdom. "Then thou shalt see, and flow together, and thine heart shall fear, and be enlarged; because the abundance of the sea shall be converted unto thee, the forces of the Gentiles shall come unto thee." (Isa. 60:5) The seas speak of humanity. Thus, the abundance of humanity shall be converted.

Paul likewise taught that the rule of the Lord Jesus Christ now extends not only to the sons of God, but to all the universe, physical and spiritual, visible and invisible. "Which he wrought in Christ, when he raised him from the dead, and set him at his own right hand in the heavenly places, Far above all principality, and power, and might, and dominion, and every name that is named, not only in this world, but also in that which is to come:" (Eph. 1:20-21)

When is the Kingdom?

Luke 17:20-21 discusses both elements of **"where"** and **"when"** concerning the kingdom of God. "And when he was demanded of the Pharisees, when the kingdom of God should come, he answered them and said, The kingdom of God cometh not with observation: Neither shall they say, Lo here! or, lo there! for, behold, the kingdom of God is within you." (The Greek phrase means:. "Stands among you")

The Wuest translation of this verse: "The Kingdom of God does not come in such a manner that one can carefully observe its approach. Neither shall they say, Look, here or there, for see, the Kingdom of God is in your midst."

The Kingdom of God was within the Pharisees but they could not recognize it, nor would they allow the King of the Kingdom to rule over them. (In the margin of the Bible: "that is, where the King is, there is the Kingdom!). Thus at the present time, and so far as the earth is concerned, where the King is and where His rule is acknowledged, is first, in the heart of the individual believer—"that Christ may dwell in your heart through faith..." (Eph. 3:17)

At that time Jesus was the sole member of the Kingdom and He was in their midst. Back to Luke, note that verse 21 states. "Neither shall they say..." The word "shall" speaks of a (near) future time. In other words, the Kingdom of God began in the days of those kings (Dan. 2:44) but would manifest on the day of Pentecost in the New Testament. We know that the Pharisees rejected Jesus as the Messiah. (Matt. 21:42-45; 26:4; 27:24-25; John 7:1; Acts 3:13-15; 4:10; 7:52; 10:39; 1 Thess. 2:14-15;).

"Not with observation" means that a person can't see or comprehend the Kingdom of God with their natural understanding or their natural power of observation, for it is spiritually discerned (John 3:3; 1 Cor. 2:14). We can't see it with our natural eyes. A person may see a great change in someone they know after that person has received Jesus Christ, but they see only a changed person, the result of the Kingdom in action. They really don't see the Kingdom, for it's hidden within the believer.

To see what God is doing in the earth today we have to peek into the spiritual realm, not read the headlines in the daily paper or listen to the 6 o'clock news. Where is that spiritual realm? It's in the hearts of men, where God first works in the firstfruits company.

Jesus as King wouldn't rule over a people or territory as other kings had done but would rule by spiritual laws within man, through the leadership of the sons of God, in the hearts of men—a rule not observed by the natural man. In His kingdom the Holy Spirit leads men. He would rule by an entirely different type of laws and rules. When would this begin? Again, the manifestation would begin on the day of Pentecost. It continues today and will continue forever and ever. (Isa. 9:7; Dan. 7:14; Rev. 22:13).

In the book of Luke, the angel told Mary, "And he shall reign over the house of Jacob for ever; and of his kingdom there shall be no end" (Luke 1:33). Jesus Christ came to establish a new world, a new type of kingdom. He didn't come just to rescue a few lost sinners. Jesus came to establish this Kingdom and to reign, along with the sons of God, as King. The excitement of the fullness of the kingdom of God radiates ahead of us as we contemplate the result of a great company of the sons of God who rule and reign in the likeness and image of the Lord Jesus Christ.

The Kingdom of God is righteousness, peace, and joy in the Holy Ghost (Rom 14:17). But members of the Kingdom exhibit these qualities differently. Some believers receive the baptism of the Holy Spirit but use only one of the nine gifts (tongues). While some Christians can walk in peace in the midst of trials and tribulation, others either haven't learned how, or strife and turmoil forever camp on their doorstep to rob them of any peace due to enter their life. The believer with true peace, on the other hand, brings this peace to others, either on a one-on-one basis or to a group as a whole. Many times I have witnessed such believers walk in a room full of people where turmoil or strife or a negative spirit prevailed and without saying a word, bring peace to that situation and to those in the room.

We can observe all ranges of joy among God's people. A mature Christian knows by his spirit what true joy is. Joy is not happiness, for happiness depends upon circumstances. True joy, however, comes from God—a joy that we can both feel and pass on to others, even in times of trouble and toil. We simply rejoice when someone with the joy of the Lord brings that joy into our life, into our day or hour of need. I've been privileged to know Christians who just seem to bubble over with the joy of the

Lord. It's a joy just to be around them. Such people, even when they tell of their problems, seem to display no sense of depression. At the other end of the spectrum, some believers host a continuous series of pity parties with negativism, fault finding and "Why me Lord" as honored guests. But it's the sons of God who, through revelation and teaching, help bring righteousness, peace and joy to others in the Kingdom.

God makes the riches of His glory known to you here and now. Your hope is not a future Kingdom out in the sky. Christ living and dwelling within you, that is your hope of glory—not Christ in heaven—not Christ in the Father—not Christ in someone else. Nor is it an escape from this corrupt world that is your hope, but Christ in you! The sons of God exist only because of their relationship to Jesus Christ. He dwells in you as God the Father dwelt in Him. (John 17:23). "The mystery which has been hidden from ages and from generations, but now has been revealed to His saints. To them God willed to make known what are the riches of the glory of this mystery among the Gentiles: which is Christ in you, the hope of glory." (Col. 1:26-27)

Light from the scriptures or from the indwelling Jesus Christ shines in the darkness of our lives. That darkness, in addition to meaning a lack of spiritual understanding, consists of those areas in our lives that do not measure up to the standard of Christ. These standards are the attributes of Jesus Christ such as love, mercy, compassion, purity, holiness, humility, light and His very life. But as long as you assign your Jesus to a place out in the sky or limit Him to some future time, rather than the reality of Christ in you, the hope of glory, then you don't have to answer to Him now. In other words, you don't feel compelled to measure up to those standards of love etc. You feel He is not looking over your shoulder, watching what you do and how you do it.

In that condition you don't have to feel convicted when faced with those standards. You feel that some day (future) He'll perfect you, and that is good enough. People say they want to show love and compassion like Jesus did but they want to choose the people to whom they show love.

From Wuest's translation of John 14:20, "In that day you shall know experientially that I am in My Father and you in me and I in you." For the disciples "that day" came on the day of Pentecost. For us, it's the day we became born again, then greatly confirmed the day we received the baptism of the Holy Spirit. "Experientially" means we come to know by experience. As long as we continue to ascribe Jesus to only the future, then we continue to procrastinate concerning any endeavor in which Jesus tries to perfect us, thinking that can came later. "I'll live my own life now. That perfection will come on the other side."

The Kingdom of God is **a present reality**. It is for us today. Many of Jesus' parables dealt with the Kingdom, especially in the book of Matthew. The Kingdom of Heaven "IS," not "shall be." We are not waiting for some future event or waiting for a literal physical appearance of Jesus to launch His Kingdom. The Jesus I know dwells within me. In that capacity He talks to me, empowers me, directs me and even corrects me. He is with me constantly. I'm not waiting to see some future Jesus with my natural eyes.

The Lord comforts us in Luke 12:32 (NAS): "Do not be afraid, little flock, for your Father has chosen gladly to give you the Kingdom." This is past tense (has chosen). How long will we continue to futurize this verse? Like the gift of the Kingdom, the conditions for our inheritance in the kingdom are also gifts from God. (Col. 1:12; 3:24; 1 Pet. 1:4).

The concept of only a futuristic kingdom leaves people with a false hope, thinking they can gain nothing in this life, while only uncertainty in the next life. Many in the church world speak often of "dying and going to heaven" as the only thing they have to look forward to. No scriptures support this expression. "And you He made alive, who were dead in trespasses and sins." (Eph. 2:1)

One of God's purposes for creation we find revealed in Zechariah. "…Thus says the LORD, who stretches out the heavens, lays the foundation of the earth, and forms the spirit of man within him:" (Zech. 12:1 NKJV) God did not create heaven as a place for man to go when he dies. God is Spirit and His purpose was to come to earth, live and express

Himself in and through a body (man), a man, whom He created, living on the earth under the umbrella and order of the Kingdom of God with Jesus Christ as King and Head. (Eph. 2:21-22)

WHY the Kingdom of God

We might add one more question to what, where, and when concerning the Kingdom of God. And that is, WHY the Kingdom, or why has God established the kingdom of God? Part of that question has been covered in the section on "What." Remember that God designed a divine method where His plan and purpose in the earth and in the universe would be carried out. This method would allow Him to manifest His nature in the earth, in mankind, so that all creation would be blessed—a plan where man could live in peace and harmony with God and with his fellow men.

The Kingdom of God enables men and women to both receive and give out the life of Jesus Christ. That Kingdom institutes a divine plan whereby man can grow into the knowledge of God, and where man can live as an overcomer. Love prevails through such a Kingdom.

Permit me to quote Earl Paulk again in his book, *The Prophetic Community,* p 15, "Why is the Kingdom of God even necessary? The obvious reason is that it is the ultimate and final solution for our world. It is the means by which God redeems mankind to Himself. But there are also some more specific purposes for the Kingdom of God." From p. 17, "The purposes of the Kingdom of God then, are to maintain order, to make God's presence known and felt among His creation, to give man an opportunity to be birthed into the Kingdom and join God's battle to regain His order on earth, and to assure us that God is always at work overcoming every other kingdom that challenges His."

Jesus said, "My sheep hear my voice, and I know them, and they follow me." (John 10:27). The Kingdom of God enables a person to learn to know the voice of God. Through prayer, meditation and communication with God, Bible study, listening to good solid preaching on the Kingdom, and obedience to the voice of God, we can become even more sensitive to His voice. If we desire to rightly discern His voice on a continuous basis however, we also have to learn how to shut out the noise of the world, literally and figuratively.

I have been married to my wife since 1950. I certainly have come to know her voice, not just to distinguish over the phone or in a crowd, but I have come to discern by the tone of her voice, how intense she is feeling about something at the time and other emotions behind her actual voice. How did I learn that? By spending quality time with her all these years. How do we learn to know the voice of Jesus Christ? The same way—by spending quality time with Him, talking to Him and listening to His voice.

What if God, through His still small voice, spoke only a faint whisper? Would we hear Him? Can we hear Him in the midst of our trials, or is our mind on our problems? How can we distinguish that whisper? By spending quality time with Him, and by entering the Most Holy Place in a frame of worship.

In my own experience, I have found that God speaks to me not only in church services and when I meditate on the scriptures or in prayer time, but when I am mowing the lawn, driving the car or many other activities. It may be a single word, a phrase, sentence or an idea that fits in with a particular piece I am writing about or am preparing to share with others or just enlightenment on the Scriptures or direction in what to do.

God so loved the world that He gave His only begotten Son. It's through His Son, the Lord Jesus Christ that those in darkness can be brought into light. God established the (true) Church as the vehicle in the Kingdom which reaches out to those still in the kingdom of darkness (Rom. 14:17; Mark 16:15; Matt. 24:14). Lastly, the Kingdom of God is a means whereby that last enemy, death, is destroyed (1 Cor. 15:26).

CHAPTER 3

▼

HOW TO ENTER THE KINGDOM

How do we enter the Kingdom of God?

We enter the kingdom of God not by death, but by a new birth. Jesus told Nicodemus, "…Verily, verily, I say unto thee, Except a man be born again (Greek meaning of this term is: born from above or born anew), he cannot see the kingdom of God" (John 3:3). Nicodemus **observed** but he did **not see**. He said, "How can that be?" Again, he spoke from the natural mind that could observe. Then in verse 5 Jesus declared, "…Verily, verily, I say unto thee, Except a man be born of water and of the Spirit, he cannot enter into the kingdom of God." The water in this verse refers to the Word of God. (1 Pet. 1:23) So we are born again by the Word of God and by the Spirit of God.

"Even when we were dead in trespasses, (God) made us alive together with Christ (by grace you have been saved), and raised us up together, and made us sit together in the heavenly places in Christ Jesus." (Eph. 2:5-6 NKJV). When we enter the Kingdom of God, we enter into an overcoming life style (John 10:10; Rom. 5:17). We now sit in heaven or a place of authority in the heavenly realm, a condition here on earth. When we were born anew, He raised us up from our mere earthly existence, from our darkness (lack of spiritual light or understanding). We were dead because of our trespasses, but now as we enter the Kingdom, we take on this new life, the life of Christ.

God, not man, decides how we enter the kingdom, and under what terms. Jesus was the greatest teacher the world has ever known, but we don't enter the Kingdom by just attempting to follow His teaching. We don't enter the Kingdom either by becoming a member of a local assembly or church or through our parents. Neither can we enter the Kingdom by natural descent or by national blood, by water baptism, or by kneeling at an altar. The natural, carnal man seeks to perform his way into the Kingdom by rituals, or by taking sacraments.

The greatest change in my life immediately after salvation (in 1974) was a deep hunger for the Word of God. I couldn't put down my Bible. For the first time in my life the Scriptures came to life. The night of my conversion, a Christian brother recommended to me that I start reading the book of Romans. I took his advice and could have sworn that letter to the Romans was written to me personally. Perhaps equally significant was knowledge in my spirit that I was saved. At once, I became aware of the presence and guidance of the Lord in my life. Through these years, not once has satan tempted me to question my salvation. My conversion experience was simply too dramatic. But that is another story.

It makes little difference if you accept Christ at your work, in your home, in a small church, or in a large crusade. It's still as an individual. Neither do we enter the Kingdom by acts of the legislature, or by forcing people. We enter by the Word of God.

The Kingdom of God or the born again experience is not an add-on. We don't see how holy or righteous we can become and then somehow let God make up the rest. That's not it at all. Our righteousness is as filthy rags. If we are born again, our old (adamic) man was crucified (past tense) with Christ. When we become a new creation in Christ Jesus, all old things are passed away. (2 Cor. 5:17) When we are born by the Spirit of God, we start fresh. Jesus said, "...That which is born of the Spirit is spirit." (John 3:6) He was talking about spiritual things. The Kingdom of God is something spiritual; therefore we must be born of the Spirit.

God seeks not a warmed-over, revised Adam. He doesn't try to improve on our old nature for no one can enter the Kingdom as they are. If we are to think spiritually and discern things spiritually, we must be born again. (1 Cor. 2:14) Mankind needs to do more than improve a little here and there in their thought life and in their actions—a series of do's and don'ts. They need a change of heart, a new birth.

In Old Testament times, the unclean could not enter the tabernacle. They first had to be cleansed. Jesus condemned the scribes and Pharisees: "Woe unto you, scribes and Pharisees, hypocrites! for ye make clean the outside of the cup and of the platter, but within they are full of extortion and excess" (Matt. 23:25). It is the inside of man that needs to be cleansed to be able to enter the Kingdom of God. Sin must be cleansed and the blood of Jesus Christ, who became the perfect sacrifice, provides the only way to cleanse it.

When we are born again (again, the Greek term means born from above), we automatically become members of the Kingdom of God, just as all babies born in the United States become citizens of the United States. Yet as a newborn baby we couldn't vote, hold an office, get married or get a driver's license. Neither could we walk, talk nor even feed ourselves. But through time, growth and maturing, we become productive citizens in the United States.

So it is in the Kingdom. We become productive members in the Kingdom of God with both added blessings and added responsibilities through a process of growth and maturing. It is very sad to say that many born-again Christians fail to grow in their spiritual life, so they remain spiritual babies. You can be a ten or twenty year old Christian and still be a spiritual baby but God doesn't desire for us to remain a baby. That new spiritual life we receive when we enter the Kingdom is the core of the blessings of the Kingdom. We are new creatures. We are now citizens of a new realm, the celestial realm, where we experience and enjoy the rights and privileges of that higher realm. Our feet are still planted on planet earth, terra firma, where we walk around, but our citizenship is in heaven or a heavenly realm.

So many Christians today resist change. They cleave to the truths that brought them to their present spiritual condition instead of cleaving to the Lord. Let us look at another's expression of our need to grow in the spirit. Quoting from *For God's Sake, Grow Up* by David Ravenhill, p 102: "(Yet) The blessing of the brazen serpent soon became a bondage to the very people it blessed. During the reign of Hezekiah, hundreds of years later, that same brazen serpent had become an object of worship, Israel's favorite idol (2 Ki. 18:4). The very object that was to testify of God became a god, an idol. Likewise, for the Pharisees, the very Scriptures that were to point them to Christ, became their obstacle to Christ. (John 5:39-40) Today fundamentalists, like the Pharisees, are in danger of becoming so focused on the written word that the Living Word is bound in their midst. No religious group or individual believer is exempt from the temptation to stop at a cherished place of blessing and settle into a comfortable theology or structure rather than moving deeper into territory that God has promised and longs to provide."

When we are born by the Spirit, we receive a new nature. We then become sharers of His divine nature (2 Pet. 1:4). We are now spirit beings where now God is our **Father.** (Rom. 8:15; Heb. 12:9) Note the father relationship in Romans 1:7 (NKJV) "…Grace to you and peace from God **our Father** and the Lord Jesus Christ." and in 1 Thessalonians 3:11, "Now may **our God and Father** Himself, and our Lord Jesus Christ, direct our way to you."

The apostle Paul wrote, "Now this I say, brethren, that flesh and blood cannot inherit the kingdom of God; neither doth corruption inherit incorruption." (1 Cor. 15:50) But if we are born again we are not of the flesh, but born of the Spirit, the incorruptible Word. Romans 8:9 declares, "But ye are not in the flesh, but in the Spirit, if so be that the Spirit of God dwell in you..."

God needs to be experienced

God needs to be experienced. The only way to know Him is by the Spirit. Paul wrote , "I am crucified with Christ." (Gal. 2:20). He wasn't just writing words or ideas that he believed to be true. He was writing from the reality of his experience with God and an ongoing, intimate relationship with the Lord Jesus Christ in which he lived and walked day by day. If believers would only embrace this truth and seek to walk it out, their lives would radically change for the better.

Paul wrote in Ephesians, "And hath raised us up together, and made us sit together in heavenly places in Christ Jesus" (Eph. 2:6) " Sit in heavenly places." Where is that? It's far above all principalities. "Far above all principality, and power, and might, and dominion, and every name that is named, not only in this world, but also in that which is to come:" (Eph. 1:21)

The word "sit" here speaks of a place of authority. "Heavenly places," on the other hand, speaks of the spiritual realm, of heaven on earth, here and now in this lifetime. It's not a heaven in the sweet by-and-by, nor is it some distant geographical place out in the sky. Paul walked in and knew the reality of that. What's more, he admonishes us to do the same. As born again Christians we have that authority now—authority over the principalities, those things that come against our mind. If we live in these heavenly places, then we are living out the nature of Christ within us. When we live in the Kingdom, our spirit and entire being is aware of living in the Kingdom. With such a nature, we love our enemies, bless them that curse us and if persecuted, we hurt not for ourselves but for those who persecute us.

When Jesus ascended, it wasn't a geographical ascension but a spiritual one where He ascended into the heavenly realm of the spirit. A cloud (not clouds) received him out of their sight. He ascended from a cloud of people (Heb. 12:1; Luke 21:27). (Or a Shekinah cloud received Him). Two men stood in white apparel. "Which also said, Ye men of Galilee, why stand ye gazing up into heaven? this same Jesus, which is taken up from you into heaven, shall so come **in like manner** as ye have seen him go into heaven." (Acts 1:11) What is the "like manner?" On the day of Pentecost He came and manifested Himself in a cloud of people. He continues to manifest Himself in man as they are born from above and filled with the Holy Spirit, ever since the day of Pentecost. Jesus had gone from the visible to the invisible realm. After the day of Pentecost He began to manifest Himself visibly through men as they were filled with the Holy Spirit.

Paul had been in the third heaven. (2 Cor 12:2) Where did he go? His body never left the planet earth. But his spirit was caught up into a heavenly sphere or realm.

Two Kingdoms

We have two kingdoms in the earth today, the Kingdom of God and the kingdom of darkness. We read in 1 Samuel 17:1-4, "Now the Philistines gathered together their armies to battle, and were gathered together at Shochoh, which belongeth to Judah, and pitched between Shochoh and Azekah, in Ephesdammim. And Saul and the men of Israel were gathered together, and pitched by the valley of Elah, and set the battle in array against the Philistines. And the Philistines stood on a mountain on the one side, and Israel stood on a mountain on the other side: and there was a valley between them. And there went out a champion out of the camp of the Philistines, named Goliath, of Gath, whose height was six cubits and a span."

"Shococh" means hedge and "Ephes-damnin" means boundary of blood. Notice that the opposing armies where camped on two different mountains, representing two opposing kingdoms. Furthermore, David slew Goliath, (1 Sam. 17:51) and just as Jesus has overcome the champion of the kingdom of darkness (satan).

Throughout the Bible, from Genesis to Revelation, God seeks to dwell with man. (1 John 1:14). In Revelation Chapter 21, we find the city, which is the bride, (the lamb's wife), comes down. In other words, she comes down (not down from the sky, but down from a higher realm) from the realm of the invisible to the realm of the visible.

The whole creation groans for the manifestation of God through the sons. (Rom 8:19) The nature and character of God, which is invisible, must become visible. Jesus was that visible expression of the invisible God. (Col. 1:15; Heb. 1:3) Now the sons of God, the leadership order, must also express that same nature and character to the rest of mankind, in shoe leather, now in this life, into a way of life that all of mankind can see, perceive, comprehend, understand, and relate to in their own life. Heaven must come to earth. Our earthly body is also sometimes referred to as the earth. The heavenly realm must become real to our body or our self.

When David came on the scene, the truth of a kingdom had expanded to include the Gentile nations on the north. "Ask of me, and I shall give thee the heathen for thine inheritance, and the uttermost parts of the earth for thy possession." (Ps. 2:8)

Seek ye first the Kingdom

Again, Matthew 6:33 exhorts us to "…seek ye first the kingdom of God, and his righteousness; and all these things shall be added unto you." We could glean a multitude of valuable nuggets and truths from this powerful verse to apply to our every day lives. All these things include paying for groceries or our light bill, and filling our car with gas. Yes, they include the material things we require to live from day to day, but also the intangible aspects of our lives.

Let me share with you a personal example. Several years ago while living in Cedar Falls, Iowa, I was working on several projects in the office of an agricultural exporter. At one particular time the workload had significantly piled up and I had gotten behind. Due to the nature of the work, I could not take the work home or work late at the office. I asked the Lord to show me how I could get caught up on my work. I was naive to think that He would reveal some systematic way to organize my work. Instead He clearly spoke to me, "Give me more of your time and I will give you mine."

In other words, He was saying, "seek first the kingdom of God and His righteousness and these other things will be added." I began to get up one hour earlier each morning to spend more time in Bible study, prayer and meditation with the Lord before I went to work. In a short time I began to cherish, enjoy and look forward to that time with the Lord. What happened to that extra workload at my office? It disappeared. That same principle has worked many times in my life since then.

If we will put the Lord first in our lives, that is, in the time we spend with Him, and obey Him, He will then supply our need. I have heard testimonies of many other people who had financial or other difficulties in their life. In some cases, they simply began to attend church more often, tithed more regularly or spent more time in personal bible study. Often as a result, their problems and difficulties greatly subsided. Some had testified that they were so busy, they first thought they didn't have time to study the Bible more (or at all) or time to go to church. This is often when we especially need to seek first the Kingdom of God and His righteousness (and **make** the time!)

Who is the Kingdom for?

Who did Jesus invite to be members of the Kingdom? He did not restrict the Kingdom to the wealthy, the religious or the powerful. In that day and culture, people thought wealth and power were a sign of God's blessings. Jesus did teach however, "And again I say unto you, It is easier for a camel to go through the eye of a needle, than for a rich man to enter into the kingdom of God." (Matt. 19:24)

According to the Lord, the tax gatherers and prostitutes would enter the Kingdom before the religious people (Matt. 21:31). The Kingdom is available for whosoever will—people of all nations, races and tongues. Jesus elevated the spiritual, emotional and physical welfare of man even above the temple rulers and the law, disregarding the religious and social cast systems of that time, to show that every person, Jew or Gentile, rich or poor, man or woman, saint or outcast could sit at God's table in the Kingdom. (Eph. 3:6)

Man, especially the Gentile or non-Jewish, had been cut off. The Jews had also cut themselves off from the blessings and favor of God by their emphasis on rituals and the traditions of men, disregarding the weightier matters. (Matt. 23:23)

If we use Jesus as our example in the Kingdom, then we welcome the "outcasts" of modern society—to come into the Kingdom, into our church services and Christian fellowship, not to assert their "rights" to be an outcast, but to be healed, spirit soul and body and to receive the Word of God. The Kingdom of God is not a bread line where God sustains the "outcasts" to live as they choose but for these people, a new birth by the Spirit of God, a transformation, a new life style where they are raised up to a place and relationship with God.

The nation of Israel was to not only bring God to its own people but also introduce God to other nations. Yet they not only oppressed their own people but also denied the Gentiles access to God. They thought the Gentiles were not worthy to receive God. (Matt 23:13,15,28) Jesus told the Pharisees and scribes that they laid heavy burdens on men's shoulders but they themselves would not move them with one of their fingers (Matt. 23:4).

When we become a spirit being, born of the Father (Heb. 12:9), we no longer retain the old nature, but receive His divine nature. (2 Pet. 1:4) That new nature becomes an integral part of us. We don't have to pray for it, wish for it, or wait until some future time. We simply allow that divine nature to expand and grow and become a comfortable part of us.

Through His Son Jesus Christ, God gives salvation as a free gift (the extent of His Kingdom) to all that will receive it. "For by grace are ye saved through faith; and that not of yourselves: it is the gift of God: Not of works, lest any man should boast." (Eph. 2:8-9)

It is the Father's good pleasure to give you the Kingdom (Luke 12:32). "Every one that thirsteth, let him come and take of the water of life freely." (Rev. 22:17) The gift of God is eternal life. Note that God gives. You can't buy the Kingdom, nor can you buy righteousness, peace, joy, salvation or the mind of Christ.

When we submit to God initially and on a daily basis, then our lifestyle and our conduct eventually will or should in turn exhibit the **glory** of the Lord. That is glory for here and now in our present lifetime. "Arise, shine; for thy light is come, and the glory of the LORD is risen upon thee. For, behold, the darkness shall cover the earth, and gross darkness the people: but the LORD shall arise upon thee, and his glory shall be seen upon thee." (Isa. 60:1-2) (See also v. 3-5.)

Let's look at two related scripture verses concerning glory and abundant life. Jesus assured us in John 10:10, "The thief cometh not, but for to steal, and to kill, and to destroy: I am come that they might have life, and that they might have it more abundantly." And Paul writes in Romans 8:18, "For I reckon that the sufferings of this present time are not worthy to be compared with the **glory** which shall be revealed in us." That is abundant spiritual life and glory **now**, in this life. What else can man do? We can repent, believing the good news of the Kingdom (Mark 1:14-15).

When Jesus instructed us to pray in this manner, "Thy kingdom come..." .in Matthew 6:10, this was not really a prayer to ask God, at some future time, to bring the Kingdom to the earth. Rather it was an affirmation that the Kingdom has already come to those areas in our lives where He is Lord. It is also an affirmation that He, now, continues to make His presence and guidance known to us in those areas of our lives in which we submit to Him as ruler. If we, for example, through the power of the Holy Spirit, have conquered an angry spirit and Jesus is the Lord of our life in that area, and makes His presence known, then the Kingdom of God has come to us in that area of our life.

Our Lifestyle in the Kingdom

Righteousness marks a believer's lifestyle in the Kingdom (Isa. 54:17). "For I say unto you, That except your righteousness shall exceed the righteousness of the scribes and Pharisees, ye shall in no case enter into the kingdom of heaven." (Matt. 5:20. See also Isa. 64:6)

The attitude of our heart in the Kingdom includes a childlike character. Jesus spoke: "And said, Verily I say unto you, Except ye be converted, and become as little children, ye shall not enter into the kingdom of heaven. Whosoever therefore shall humble himself as this little child, the same is greatest in the kingdom of heaven." (Matt. 18:3-4) I don't believe Jesus stated this (v. 3) as a legalistic requirement but a principle. Without that child-like principle working in our life, we cannot advance to or enjoy the fullness of the Kingdom.

The term "child-like" does not mean or imply being or acting "childish". We suggest a vast difference between the two terms. One who is childish performs foolish, immature acts as a child might. They usually demonstrate selfishness, demand their own way and often whine or complain. An adult believer who is childish may ignore people they really should be fellowshipping with.

If we are childlike, then we are teachable, meek, or willing and eager to learn and to receive instructions. We are open and willing to change from our own ways to the ways of God. Children are trusting, they are quick to forgive and forget, and they give themselves wholly to those who have earned their respect. We shouldn't get angry at correction, especially if it is given in a humble spirit. The truth is, as I'm sure you know, we really shouldn't get angry at correction, even if someone corrects us in the wrong spirit. This is part of the power of the gospel that we can behave like Jesus who even when treated unfairly did not retaliate. This is central to spiritual growth. We must first recognize a need to be taught. Jesus, via the Holy Spirit within us, continues to teach us. Therefore, we must continue to learn. Moses, for example, was a very meek person, willing to be taught by his father-in-law Jethro and by God. Considering he is looked upon as one of the greatest leaders in the Bible, he demonstrated a quality needed by all leaders. We certainly need more leaders to arise in the Body to help lead the masses out of the wilderness.

Continuing now in Matthew 18:6-7, "But whoso shall offend one of these little ones which believe in me, it were better for him that a millstone were hanged about his neck, and that he were drowned in the depth of the sea. Woe unto the world because of offences! for it must needs be that offences come; but woe to that man by whom the offence cometh!"

In this story we have two persons, "the child," who is the greatest in the kingdom of heaven and "that man" who Jesus refers to, as so offensive he should be drowned. He is also offensive to the child of the Kingdom. Both of these personalities are in you and me. "That man" is the soulish, natural man, who lives by his senses, is selfish, self centered and incapable of knowing or understanding the things and ways of God. (1 Cor. 2:14).

The second person, "the child," we can't see with our natural eyes for it is our spiritual or inner being, the seed of Christ—Christ in you the hope of glory. The little child is the spiritual man who has put on the mind of Christ and bears the image of God.

A good many years ago, my wife and I attended a family Christmas party for a group in which she was a member. Several children sang songs or recited poems. They then asked if anyone else had a song or poem. One little boy about four years old got up and sang "Rudoph the Red Nosed Reindeer." He had a good voice but he didn't know all words to the song. Without hesitation or the slightest embarrassment, never missing a beat or even lowering his voice, he simply hummed the parts he didn't know. He received a big ovation. That is being child-like. You see, as adults, we set such legalistic standards and exact boundary lines for our behavior that we squelch any freedom we might have to act from our spirit, or the pure child within us. That boy sung from his heart, just as if he was singing to himself.

A childlike person willingly listens to the opinions and doctrines of others, even those they don't agree with. They likewise examine their own doctrines from time to time. The word "doctrine" isn't a negative word nor does it imply a "far out" or man-made teaching as we may have thought in the past. The word "doctrine" (KJV) in the New Testament comes from two Greek words. The first word is *didache* meaning "that which is taught (Matt 7:28) or (b) the act of teaching (e.g. Mark 4:2). The other Greek word, *didaskalla,* also translates doctrine and means (a) that which is taught (Matt. 15:9) or (b) teaching, instruction (e.g. Rom 12:7). A note from Vine's Expository Dictionary of New Testament Words states that both these words are used in passive and active senses (i.e. the act of teaching and what is taught).

Jesus Christ produces His life or lifestyle in us and through us. We make up the living vehicle in which He can express Himself *to* the rest of humanity, and eventually *in* all humanity. Through Christ mankind can now begin to sense this divine purpose of life.

Holiness in the Kingdom

Throughout the churches of the United States there are two things that are killing or destroying the seed of the Word of God, and as a result hinder the growth of the Kingdom of God. That is, the seed of Christ has no chance to grow and mature. These two things are (1) legalism and (2) license, or law and lust. Paul dealt with both of these in the book of Galatians.

A few decades ago many of our local churches became bound by legalism. When they broke the chains off that bondage, however, they couldn't handle the freedom. Believers then began to do anything they felt "led by the spirit to do," even mating up with their "spiritual spouse." They let their children do their own thing. "Take off all restraints, let them express themselves" was a popular teaching, even in the church. God, now in the 21st Century, calls us to repentance from these attitudes and lifestyles, into pure holiness. "But take heed to yourselves, lest your hearts be weighed down with carousing, drunkenness, and cares of this life, and that Day come on you unexpectedly." (Luke 21:34 NKJV)

We need to constantly pursue righteousness and a life of holiness in the Kingdom. "But seek for (aim at and strive after) first of all His kingdom, and His righteousness [His ways of doing and being right], and then all these things taken together will be given you besides." (Matt. 6:33 AMP)

To walk as an overcomer in the Kingdom we clothe ourselves with humility. (Matt. 5:3). We do not overcome by our own effort but by the blood of the Lamb and the Word of our testimony (Rev. 12:11). An over-comer is one who is transformed day by day, from glory to glory. Life style in the Kingdom includes doing the will of the Father (Matt. 7:21-23). A believer in the kingdom also demonstrates a disciplined lifestyle. We speak of this in detail elsewhere.

How does a person who walks in the Kingdom handle tribulation? He doesn't turn back, but presses on through tribulation and trials. "The law and the prophets were until John: since that time the kingdom of God is preached, and every man presseth into it." (Luke 16:16) "Every man" indicates a personal responsibility. Once we enter the Kingdom, we then, with the presence and anointing and strength of the Lord, begin to build our new life.

Tribulations come to us, largely through our own mind, or how our mind handles and perceives the circumstances that surround us. If we drive to work each day in heavy traffic, we are subject to tribulation. At our place of work we subject ourselves to tribulation. When we shop in the grocery or discount store, we are subject to tribulation. Notice that I said "subject to". If we easily get upset at what people do or say, then we will have tribulation. On the other hand, if we are calm, peace-loving, and forgiving, then we will have less tribulation. Jesus warned us, "...In the world ye shall have tribulation: but be of good cheer; I have overcome the world." Notice that He said He has overcome the "world," not "tribulation." The "great tribulation" however, spoken of in the Bible (Matt. 24:21), we need not fear, as the fear mongers would have you to believe. That "great tribulation" was fulfilled in A.D. 70 with the fall of Jerusalem.

Building our Life in the Kingdom

Let us examine two verses of scripture. First, "Unless the LORD builds the house, They labor in vain who build it; Unless the LORD guards the city, The watchman stays awake in vain." (Ps. 127:1 NKJV)

And second, Psalm 121:3-5 NKJV, "He will not allow your foot to be moved; He who keeps you will not slumber. Behold, He who keeps Israel shall neither slumber nor sleep. The LORD is your keeper; The LORD is your shade at your right hand."

In the first verse above, the "house" refers to our entire being—our life, our spiritual growth, and our attitude. Unless the Lord builds our house, which is our life, we labor in vain, for what we try to do to shape our life in our own strength and our own willpower will have no lasting result or viable fruit. It's as straw. It brings no spiritual life to us nor to those we contact. It's easily town down by storms or winds; it's like building a house on sand. We not only need a good foundation (1 Cor. 10:4; 1 Cor. 3:11), but we also need ongoing spiritual guidance in our growth. The word "city" from the above verse means a people (Heb. 11:10, 16; Rev 3:12; Rev 21:23). The Lord guards our mind by our conscience. The Holy Spirit reminds us when we go wrong by guarding us from receiving wrong teaching and from negative thoughts and thoughts of condemnation. If He doesn't guard them, we will guard them in vain.

We see something similar concerning the Lord as a refuge in the building the body of Christ in the following scripture. "For thou hast been a strength to the poor, a strength to the needy in his distress, a refuge from the storm, a shadow from the heat, when the blast of the terrible ones is as a storm against the wall." (Isa. 25:4) The NAS reads, "...for the breath of the ruthless is like a rainstorm against a wall."

If we have been born again, we have entered the Kingdom of God. Now it is time to grow and live as productive members of the Kingdom. We won't fold our hands and say, "Now that I'm saved, that's all there is to it." No, we will move forward in the Kingdom of God. In fact, if we don't move forward in the Kingdom, we're actually moving backward.

Taking lessons from the Scriptures, we can safely say that through much tribulation, we enter the Kingdom of God. Paul was caught up to the third heaven but his feet never left the earth. Likewise the sons of God do not escape tribulations but walk as victors through them. (The "great tribulation" occurred in 70 AD.) They are not to be burned in a fiery furnace but walk as the Hebrew children with one like the son of God through the fire of the Holy Spirit, to come forth liberated and victorious without the smell of smoke upon them. They are not to be eaten by the lions (satan and his demons) but to stand as Daniel, unharmed as an angel shut their mouths. They are not to die of thirst but to drink like Elijah did from the brook of the living water. They are not to perish from hunger (for the Word) but to supply the woman (church) with meal and oil. They are not to be slain by its Jezebel (Babylon) but to conquer her prophets and destroy her altars, proclaiming rain upon the earth.

CHAPTER 4

▼

THREE EXPERIENCES OF THE BELIEVER.

Man is a three part being. He is a spirit, he possesses a soul (mind, will and emotions) and he lives in a body. Jesus told Nicodemus, "...except a man be born again (Gr: born from above or born anew), he cannot see the kingdom of God" (John 3:3) Our spirit has been saved (the day we were born anew or again), our soul is in the process of being saved, and our body shall be saved. "(God) Who delivered us from so great a death, and doth deliver; in whom we trust that he will yet deliver us." (2 Cor. 1:10) Our initial salvation (of our spirit) is by our confession of faith. "That if thou shalt confess with thy mouth the Lord Jesus, and shalt believe in thine heart that God raised him from the dead, thou shalt be saved." (Rom. 10:9)

God saves our soul through a process. "And be not conformed to this world: but be ye transformed by the renewing of your mind, that ye may prove what is that good, and acceptable, and perfect, will of God." (Rom.

12:2) Other witnesses: "Therefore lay aside all filthiness and overflow of wickedness, and receive with meekness the implanted word, which is able to save your souls." (Jas. 1:21 NKJV) (Ps. 23:3) (See also Phil. 3:10-14).

Paul writes to the Philippians, "[For my determined purpose is] that I may know Him—that I may progressively become more deeply and intimately acquainted with Him, perceiving and recognizing and understanding [the wonders of His Person] more strongly and more clearly. And that I may in that same way come to know the power outflowing from His resurrection [which it exerts over believers]; and that I may so share His sufferings to be continually transformed [in spirit into His likeness even] to His death, [in the hope] That if possible I may attain to the [spiritual and moral resurrection [that lifts me] out from among the dead [even while in the body]." (Phil. 4:10-11 AMP)

The soul includes the mind, emotions and will of man; in other words, what he thinks, what he feels and what he wants. God is now delivering our soul. "Receiving the end of your faith, even the salvation of your souls." (1 Pet. 1:9) The way we think about things and circumstances is what God needs to save or transform.

Quoting from *Prevail* by Kelly Varner, p 65, "The greatest hindrance to your Christian walk is the way that you think! The devil is not your problem. It's what you think about the devil! Circumstances are not the issue, but rather what we think about those circumstances."

Let us quote form the Amplified Bible, "For those who are according to the flesh and controlled by its unholy desires, set their mind on and pursue those things which gratify the flesh. But those who are according to the Spirit and [controlled by the desires] of the Spirit, set their minds on and seek those things which gratify the (Holy) Spirit. Now the mind of the flesh [which is sense and reason without the Holy Spirit] is death—death that comprises all the miseries arising from sin, both here and hereafter. But the mind of the (Holy) Spirit is life and soul-peace [both now and forever]. [That is] because the mind of the flesh—with its carnal thoughts and purposes—is hostile to God; for it does not submit itself to God's law, indeed it cannot." (Rom. 8:5-7 AMP)

Our body as well as our spirit and our soul have to be saved (redeemed). Romans 8:23 states, "And not only they, but ourselves also, which have the firstfruits of the Spirit, even we ourselves groan within ourselves, waiting for the adoption, to wit, the redemption of our body."

At the moment of regeneration, (the new birth), a person receives a new heart and a new nature. In justification, man receives a new standing that includes 1. The remission of the penalty of death. 2. The restoration to favor with God, and 3. The impartation of righteousness.

The *source* of justification is the grace of God (Rom 3:24; Titus 3:7), whereas the *ground* of justification is the blood of Jesus Christ. He paid for this righteousness given to us (Rom. 3:24; 5:9; Heb. 9:22) through His death on the cross. In justification our sins weren't excused, but punished, and then removed through the person and work of the Lord Jesus Christ. In this justification, man stands before the Judge (God) and receives a sentence of acquittal. We receive this by faith (Rom. 8:1). The word "justification" does not mean "just as if I hadn't sinned" as we may have been taught in the past. God is a just and holy God and cannot excuse sin or look on it lightly. He dealt with it. Let us read Romans 5:1, "Therefore being justified by faith, we have peace with God through our Lord Jesus Christ:"

We are saved, not by His death, but by His life. Romans 5:10 makes this clear, "For if, when we were enemies, we were reconciled to God by the death of his Son, much more, being reconciled, we shall be saved (justified) by his life." Because of Adam's sin, death has reigned in us or we have sinned. Romans 5:17 tells us, "For if by one man's offence death reigned by one; much more they which receive abundance of grace and of the gift of righteousness shall reign in life by one, Jesus Christ." Without the shedding of blood there is no remission of sin. (Heb. 9:22) A man had to die to pay for the sin of man. Jesus paid that price; He died on our behalf.

The construction and function of the tabernacle in the wilderness, even in much of the detail, was a type and shadow of the way in which the Kingdom of God operates. In the Old Testament economy, God dwelt **among the** people. God told Moses, "And let them make me a sanctuary; that I may dwell **among** them." (Exod. 25:8) In contrast, in the New Testament, God, via the Holy Spirit, dwells **within** the believers (John 17:21, 23). "To whom God would make known what is the riches of the glory of this mystery among the Gentiles; which is Christ in you, the hope of glory:" (Col. 1:27)

The Three Feasts

In the Old Testament, God instructed the Israelites to observe three feasts every year. "Three times in a year shall all thy males appear before the Lord thy God in the place which he shall choose; in the feast of unleavened bread (feast of Passover, Lev. 23:6), and in the feast of weeks (Pentecost, Lev. 23:16), and in the feast of tabernacles (Lev. 23:34) and they shall not appear before the Lord empty." (Deut.16: 16) Man gives offerings and service, as he is able. Deuteronomy 16:17 states, "Every man shall give as he is able, according to the blessing of the LORD thy God which he hath given thee." God will meet man those three times.

Those feasts that took place in the Old Testament economy of people in the natural, illustrated types and shadows of a true and real spiritual experience for the individual believer and for the body of Christ as a whole today. When God meets man in the first dimension (Passover experience), man sees Jesus as His Savior. In the second dimension (Pentecostal experience) He is Christ the Anointed One. The third feast is a harvest feast. In this dimension (feast of tabernacles experience) He is Lord, the Lord of the Harvest.

When we were first saved, (Passover or salvation experience) we looked to Jesus as our Savior, and this is proper. But when we receive the baptism of the Holy Spirit, we no longer think of Jesus just a savior but as the Christ, which means the Anointed One. God anointed Jesus Christ to preach the gospel (Luke. 4:18). Believers also have an anointing from the Holy One indicating that this anointing renders them holy, separating them to God. It relates to the Holy Spirit who enables the believer to possess knowledge of the truth. (1 John 2:20,27)

The tabernacle in the wilderness and the one that Solomon built had three main compartments: the outer court, (for all Israel), the Holy Place (for the priests), and the Most Holy Place (which the High Priest entered once a year. (Exod. 40:1-9) The outer court had natural light, which corresponds to natural understanding and to those who have only had the salvation experience or have lived in the 30-fold realm.

The Holy Place possessed the artificial light of the candlestick (lampstand) (Exod. 27:20; 40:4, 25), which many Bible scholars relate to the seven Spirits of God (Isa. 11:2). This light also corresponds to the light (understanding) given by the Holy Spirit to the believer who receives the baptism of the Holy Spirit with evidence of speaking in tongues or one of the other gifts of the Spirit. That evidence of tongues can also lie dormant for a time within certain individuals. This is also called the Pentecostal Experience or the 60-fold realm. (Matt. 13:1-8)

The Most Holy Place had the divine light of God, the uncreated Light (Lev. 16:2; Rev. 22:5), corresponding to divine understanding (revelation knowledge) or the experience of the believer walking in the 100-fold realm. God is light (1 John. 1:5). When the believer has passed the 30 and 60 fold realms and pressed on into the 100-fold realm, he begins to receive this divine understanding. The believer now walks in a significant part of the Feast of Tabernacles Experience. (1 John. 1:5)

The first two experiences, salvation and the baptism of the Holy Spirit, God presents as free gifts. Admittedly, some struggle to receive the gift of the Holy Spirit, but it's still free. A person must seek and press into or needs to put more effort into walking in this third experience. Such a process we must walk out.

The believer walking in the salvation or 30-fold experience concerns himself with regeneration, water baptism, sanctification (set apart), justification and divine healing. He relates to Jesus Christ as Savior and Sanctifier. In the outer court the water of the Word cleanses the believer (Eph. 5:26-27).

In the Holy Place, the believer has received the baptism of the Holy Spirit. Here he walks by the light of the candlestick (lamp stand) (Exod. 25:31-40). We note that light is the nature of God and Christ is called the Light (John 3:14-21). The nature of Jesus is revealed through the fruit of the Spirit (Gal. 5:22-23), while the ministry of Jesus is received through the gifts of the Spirit (1 Cor. 12:8-10). In this realm the believer operates through the fruit of the Spirit or extended nature of Jesus.

In the Holy of Holies, the third level of Christian maturity, or 100-fold realm, we find the fullness of the Spirit (John 3:34) and the fullness of our inheritance, which is all things in Christ Jesus (Eph 1:3; 2 Pet. 1:4). From this realm, Jesus Christ ministers in a realm of no limitations or failures, no sickness, and no death because there is no curse. The floor of the Holy of Holies in the tabernacle was of earth, showing us that an end- time people of God here in the earth will experience this dimension as they experience the Feast of Tabernacles.

Like the Head, Jesus Christ, a glorious company and (true) church will receive the Spirit without measure (John 3:24). The Most Holy Place was 10 x 10 x 10 cubits representing the 1000-year kingdom age.

We might stop here to relate these realms to the Kingdom of God. Believers who walk in the 30-fold realm are definitely some of the subjects of the Kingdom. Most are happy in their role and don't desire to move on higher in the Kingdom. In balance however, we must state that many of these with only a salvation experience (30-fold) lack a true vision of the Kingdom of God and don't understand God's purpose for their lives. Many have been erroneously taught that there is nothing beyond salvation.

Likewise those in the 60-fold realm dwell as subjects of the Kingdom and many of these are also content in their role in the Kingdom, not wanting or desiring to move higher. Don't discount these subjects of the Kingdom. Many prove faithful and serve the Lord well in their realm. Some believers, however, seek to move higher into the 100-fold realm of leadership, the realm of sonship. Sadly, I believe that only a small percentage of the believers currently walk in this highest realm of the spirit.

Jesus said, "...I am the way, the truth, and the life; no man cometh unto the Father, but by me. (John. 14:6) Again, these three (the way, truth, and life) correspond to the three experiences of the believer; also to Jesus, the Holy Spirit, and God the Father. Jesus is the way, the only way to the Father. He is the Door. (John 10:9) By none other can one be saved. (Acts. 4:12) He is our sacrificial Lamb on the brazen altar.

In the outer court of the tabernacle the babes drink milk (Heb. 5:13). In the Holy Place young men (1 John 2:13) eat meat, but in the Holiest of Holies, sons partake of the hidden manna (Rev. 2:17), which is the Word of God, or secret things of God and life revealed, or revelation knowledge, Christ in you, the hope of glory. (Col. 1:27)

In Matthew 20:16 Jesus said, "...for many be called, but few be chosen." The called are "those of" or those who belong to the 30-fold or salvation realm. The chosen fall into the 60-fold realm, with the baptism of the Holy Spirit. The SENT ones dwell in the higher 100-fold realm. "And Moses SENT them to spy out the land..." (Num. 13:17). And in John. 20:21 Jesus said, "...peace be unto you, as my Father hath SENT me, even so SEND I you."

It is Expedient That I Go Away

Jesus lived on the earth under the old covenant. But He began to usher in the important part of the new covenant when He told His disciples, "...It is expedient for you that I go away..." (John 16:7) The key to New

Testament teaching is that the Holy Spirit would live IN man, that He would guide and direct him into all truths. (John 16:13; 17:21,23)

Many Christians would envy the disciples who were able to follow Jesus for three and a half years, to listen to Him speak, to be personally taught by Him, to witness His miracles and to see Him raise people from the dead. Remember though, He startled His disciples when He told them in John 16:7, "Nevertheless I tell you the truth; **It is expedient for you that I go away**: for if I go not away, the Comforter will not come unto you; but if I depart, I will send him unto you." The NKJV and NAS read: "...it is to your advantage..." Wuest—"...it is advantageous.."; Phillips—"...it is a good thing...."; NIV—"...it is for your good...".

Vine's Expository Dictionary states that the word "expedient" comes from the Greek word *sumphero*,...to be an advantage, profitable, expedient, (not merely 'convenient'). (Translated "it is profitable" in Matt. 5:29, 30; 18:6; "to profit withal" in 1 Cor. 12:7).

Jesus also taught that power would come from the Holy Spirit to not only help with power over our sins but power to control our soul and body. (Acts 1:8, "But ye shall receive power after that the Holy Ghost is come upon you...") In John 16:13, we read, "Howbeit when he, the Spirit of truth, is come, he will guide you into all truth...." Jesus said, "...thy word is truth." (John 17:17) It is through the Baptism of the Holy Spirit that the Scriptures (Word) are opened up to the spiritual understanding of the believer. Praying in tongues really helps the believer receive revelation knowledge.

Though He was the greatest teacher the world has ever known, the perfect example in every aspect of His earthly life, Jesus said that it was expedient that He go away. Why? So that He could send the Holy Spirit, the Comforter, on the other side of His death and the shedding of His blood of the New Covenant. The Holy Spirit would then be the believer's constant teacher, 24 hours of every day.

People I know have described trips to the Holy Land where they saw Christians from the U.S. kneel down and kiss the ground because "that is where Jesus walked." They also say, "If only I had been living when Jesus lived and was able to touch the hem of His garment. Oh, if I could have walked the shores of Galilee with Him."

Such an attitude misses the key of the gospels—yes, even misses the key to the resurrection and does not show gratitude and appreciation for Jesus' sacrifice. How unfortunate that the average Christian looks either to the historic Jesus, where they could see, touch, and hear Him in person or they look to a future Jesus whom they say will come in person so they can hear Him speak in person, in the flesh. But I tell you a truth, if that is your vision, you have missed the basic teaching of the New Testament (Covenant). I pray that you will meditate on the following until it becomes part of your consciousness. If you are born from above, the Holy Spirit is NOW. He guides you, directs you, moment by moment, if necessary, even in your thoughts. As long as you're leading an obedient, consecrated, holy life, He will continue to speak to you. He reaches and communicates with your spirit. This is Christ in you. (Col. 1:27)

It was expedient (to their advantage) that Jesus leave the natural realm where His disciples could see, hear, and touch Him in person, to go to the Father, to the spiritual, invisible realm. Only then could He send the Holy Spirit to be with them always—where the laws would be written on their hearts—where they could operate and live a changed life under the New Covenant. In this dimension or on this level they could no longer feel His natural touch and hear His natural voice, but they could now perceive His spiritual touch, could hear His voice 24 hours a day with their spiritual ear, and could see Him with their spiritual eyes. They would also experience the true life itself of the Spirit of Jesus Christ flowing from within them out to others.

Judas (not Iscariot) had spoken to Jesus. "Jesus answered and said unto him, If a man love me, he will keep my words: and my Father will love him, and we will come unto him, and make our abode with him." (John 14:23) "And what agreement hath the temple of God with idols? for ye are the temple of the living God; as God hath said, I will dwell in them, and walk in them; and I will be their God, and they shall be my people."(2 Cor. 6:16) God is really saying, "I will dwell in them and live in them. I will walk in them." God speaks to us or our spirit. But His Spirit is also in us. This is Christ in you.

Jesus prayed to the Father in John 17:21-22 and declared, "That they all may be (under the New Covenant) one; as thou, Father, art in me, and I in thee, that they also may be one in us: that the world may believe that thou hast sent me. And the glory which thou gavest me I have given them; that they may be (under the New Covenant) one, even as we are one" (parentheses this author). What is this saying? That under the New Covenant, we, the believers, are becoming one with one another just as Jesus and the Father are one and that we become as one in Jesus Christ and in the Father. The following verse 23 in the Amplified states, "I in them and You in Me, in order that they may become one *and* perfectly united, that the world may know *and* [definitely] recognize that You sent Me, and that You have loved them [even] as You have loved Me."

With Christ in us and us in Christ, we have His life and we have the life of the Father, a life that dwells and operates in our very being. As that life becomes one with Jesus and one with the Father, people should begin to see not us, but the Christ within us. Then as we become one with each other, the world will know and recognize that the Father sent Jesus and that He loves them. We Christians and the life we lead, is often the only Jesus that people of the world will see.

This life (*zoe* or spiritual life), comes from the Father, but is given to His Son. "For as the father hath life *(zoe)* in himself, so hath he given to the Son to have life *(zoe)* in himself." (John 5:26) Jesus claimed, "I and my father are one" (John 10:30). Here we distinguish "spiritual" life from our "natural" life.

"...I came that they may have *and* enjoy life *(zoe)* and have it in abundance—to the full, till it overflows" (John. 10:10 AMP.). That very life *(zoe)* of God the Father then becomes life in the many-membered son, not just life to possess, but life to give to others—to the world—that the

Kingdom of God, including God's will, may manifest itself in the earth—in the everyday life of first, the sons of God, then the other believers. "Thy kingdom come..." (Matt. 6:10).

CHAPTER 5

▼

HOW TO WALK IN THE KINGDOM

Can we walk the straight and narrow path of the Kingdom? Yes, but that's not enough. Can we walk and lead a Kingdom life that others would both desire and be able to follow, a walk that manifests the Christ within us? Can our Kingdom walk positively affect those we contact? Definitely yes. Such an active walk demonstrates a character of the sons of God.

We usually walk according to what we believe, whether good or bad, right or wrong, true or false. We may know much of what the Scriptures tell us about walking the Christian life or in the Kingdom, but it takes time (often years) and effort to put all that into practice. For some, the truth does little more than tickle their ears. They hear or read a good Word and say, "That's great", but then fail to put it into practice. James warns against being hearers and not doers of the Word. (Jas. 1:22)

"Our Kingdom walk" means not what we do on Sunday morning or what we do when we feel "spiritual" or when we experience goose bumps. Rather, it's our daily activity, even our thought patterns. Our walk includes our response to God dealing with us in our everyday life. We need to subject ourselves to the King. What soldier would be able to fulfill his duties without being obedient to his commanding officer?

The Kingdom of God is not a futuristic Disney World out in the sky. Neither is it a fantasy land that we visit (walk in) once in a while. It's not just future. It's a present reality, something we walk in right now. Jesus said, "The kingdom of God is within you" (Luke 17:21). The Kingdom stood in their midst in the person of Jesus Christ. He is the Kingdom of God on the earth.

The word "walk" translated in much of the New Testament from the Greek word *peripateo*, is used in a physical sense in the synoptic gospels (first three gospels) (except Mark 7:5). But figuratively the word "walk" signifies the whole round of the activities of the individual life, whether of the unregenerate (Eph. 4:17) or of the believer (1 Cor. 7:17; Col. 2:6). It is applied as well to the word "conduct." Wuest Expanded Translation often translated the Greek word *peripateo* as "ordered behavior" This is in the sense of an arrangement, pattern or distinguishing characteristic. We will return to this later in this chapter.

In Galatians 2:14 we also have the Greek word *orthopodeo*, meaning to walk in a straight path (*orthos*—straight, *pous*—a foot) signifying a course of conduct by which one leaves a straight path for others to follow. Concerning Paul's rebuke of Peter, "But when I say that they walked not uprightly according to the truth of the gospel..." The NAS version reads: "...were not straightforward." The remainder of the verse from the NAS states: "I said to Cephas in the presence of all, 'If you, being a Jew, live like the Gentiles, and not like the Jews, how is it that you compel the Gentiles to live like Jews?'" His talk to Cephas (Peter) continues through verse 21.

How Not to Walk

To gain insight into the Scriptures on walking, we might first look at the negative side. Romans 8:1 makes reference to the flesh: "There is now no condemnation to them which are in Christ Jesus who **walk not after**

(NKJV: according to) **the flesh,** but after the Spirit" Verse 4 states, "That the righteousness of the law might be fulfilled in us, **who walk not after the flesh** but after the Spirit." The natural man who walks after the flesh walks in bondage and corruption, in the realm of sin and death, in alienation from God. His only escape is to be born again.

Wuest comments the following on Romans 8:1, "The words, 'who walk not after the flesh but after the Spirit' are descriptive of the Christian, an identifying characteristic, that is true of every child of God. 'Flesh' is the indwelling evil nature. 'Spirit' is the Holy Spirit. 'After' is *kata*, whose root meaning is 'down,' which suggests **domination.** A Christian is one who orders his behavior in such a way that it be not **dominated** by the evil nature but by the Holy Spirit."

"But I say, walk *and* live habitually in the (Holy) Spirit—responsive to *and* controlled and guided by the Spirit; then you will certainly not gratify the cravings *and* desires of the flesh—of human nature without God." (Gal. 5:16 AMP)

The apostle Peter expands on the flesh walk, "...them that **walk after the flesh** in the lust of uncleanness, and despise government." (2 Pet. 2:10) (NAS version reads: despise authority). Peter explains how we walked before salvation. "For the time past...when we **walked** in lasciviousness, lusts, excess of wine, reveling, banquetings, and abominable idolatries." (1 Pet. 4:3).

In 1 Corinthians, Chapter 3 Paul rebuked the Corinthians church, calling them carnal and as babes in Christ. Verse 3: "For ye are yet carnal: for whereas there is among you envying, and strife and divisions, are ye not carnal and **walk as men?**" The Amplified Bible reads: "mere (unchanged) men." Paul had fed them milk rather than meat (v. 2) and declares that they were still unable to accept the meat of the Word. Why? Because they were walking as worldly, unregenerate men. It is quite likely that they did not properly digest the "milk of the Word" by obeying it or walking it out.

Paul, after writing about our earthly tabernacle, assured the Corinthians, "For we walk by faith, not by sight." (2 Cor. 5:7) Walking by sight (AMP: appearance) is walking by what we comprehend only through our senses. "This I say therefore, and testify in the Lord, that ye henceforth **walk not as other Gentiles walk,** in the vanity of their mind." (Eph. 4:17) The Amplified reads,"…that you must no longer live as the heathen (the Gentiles) do in their permissiveness—in the folly, vanity and emptiness of their souls and the futility—of their minds." Such minds obviously don't submit to, nor are they trained by the Spirit.

We read in Psalm 1:1, "Blessed is the man that walketh not in the counsel of the ungodly, nor standeth in the way of sinners, nor sitteth in the seat of the scornful." The Amplified reads, "Blessed—Happy—fortunate, prosperous and enviable—is the man who walks *and* lives not in the counsel of the ungodly [following their advice, their plans and purposes] nor stands [submissive and inactive] in the path where sinners walk, nor sits down [to relax and rest] where the scornful [and mockers] gather."

The ungodly comprise those who don't know God personally and who follow an ungodly lifestyle. The natural man never learns how to walk in peace, holiness, faith and spiritual victory. He obviously can't conquer his own flesh. He receives his guidance from his own experiences and the counsel (advice) of the ungodly. By the world's standards, many people appear successful. Yet, until they are born again (born from above) they have little access to divine guidance in their walk. Admittedly, for the child of God, it takes time to learn how to walk by faith, how to be led by the Spirit—but it is a walk with God who gives perfect peace and in whose hands we can place our trust.

The Psalmist writes, "The Lord is my rock and my fortress, and my deliverer…" (Ps. 18:2) "The sorrows of death compassed me, and the floods of ungodly men made me afraid." (Ps. 18:4) Floods are the ways and the philosophies of the world that would destroy our Christian life. They are the lies of the enemy. How do we get anchored on the Rock (Jesus Christ), in the midst of these floods? We heed the Word of God.

For the most part, God gives us the power to walk in what we see by our spirit. "For it is God which worketh in you both to will and to do of his good pleasure." (Phil. 2:13) In other words, after God reveals to us a particular spiritual truth, He then gives us the power to walk it out. Some revelations we receive however may call for us to wait for the next generation or "move of God" to walk out. For example, God allowed Moses to see the Promised Land, but he didn't get to cross over in his lifetime. It was Joshua, one of the next "generation" who crossed over. Martin Luther didn't receive the privilege to walk out all that he saw. And many in the Latter Rain movement of 1948 didn't get to walk out all that they saw, for they had to pass on some to the next "generation" of believers. We are now in that generation and now reap some of benefits of what God revealed to those ahead of us.

The average Christian has barely tapped the limitless resources of God in the area of guidance of his daily walk. God can do exceedingly abundantly above all that we ask or think. How? By the power that works in us, the same power that raised Jesus from the dead. (Eph. 3:20). The Scriptures, of course, are the basic guidelines. Any additional guidance we receive directly from God however, should line up with the Scriptures.

The person, believer or non-believer, who operates from his or her carnal mind, is limited to making choices as to **where** and **how** to walk. Such a mind limits the person's walk to the realm of darkness. Darkness speaks of the lack of spiritual understanding. The carnal, natural man can't walk in the light, in the heavenly realm of the Spirit. He is totally incapable of such. He forever looks to the flesh for guidance. He can't know the things of God, which include how to walk in the Kingdom and how to be guided by the Holy Spirit, for the things of God are spiritually discerned. (1 Cor 2:14)

The Amplified renders this verse: "But the natural, nonspiritual man does not accept *or* welcome *or* admit into his heart the gifts *and* teachings *and* revelations of the Spirit of God, for they are folly (meaningless nonsense) to him; and he is incapable of knowing them—of progressively recognizing, understanding and becoming better acquainted with them—because they are spiritually discerned *and* estimated *and* appreciated."

Proverbs 28:19 states, "He that tilleth his land shall have plenty of bread: but he that followeth after vain persons (NKJV: frivolity; NAS: "...follows empty pursuits..." AMP: "...follows worthless people...") shall have poverty enough."

To follow frivolity (vain) is to walk after or according to the ways and philosophies of vain people. Controlling our thoughts and actions to walk in the Spirit requires daily effort. Thoughts that take up a lot of our time may not necessarily be evil in themselves but rob from the time we should be communing with the Lord. The word "bread" in this verse speaks of food, both natural and spiritual. In our spare time, or in the time we drive to and from work, do we spend time with the Lord or do we think about our work, about some program we saw on TV, or our hobbies? These can rob our time with the Lord and can be the biggest time wasters.

Jesus taught in Mark 4 that if we don't weed out the thorns and thistles in our lives, they would choke the Word. Instead, we allow or purposely dwell on good, pleasant, productive, positive thoughts to enter our mind. Philippians 4:8 tells us, "If there be any praise, think on these things." The weeds speak of false teaching, false doctrines, unbelief, doubt, and fear. "Water by the Word" means to allow the crop to grow—or allow these truths to grow. We walk these truths out when we practice them in our daily lives. "Empty pursuits" means to spend time on useless thoughts and activity, ones that lead to nowhere.

If the Lord has revealed to us many truths of the 60 or 100 fold realms and we have learned to walk in either of these, why should we fall back to walk in the 30-fold realm? This doesn't mean that after we have reached the Pentecostal realm (31-60 fold) that we can't minister salvation or simple helps to another brother or sister. Neither does it mean that once we reach the 100-fold realm that we ignore the gifts of the 60-fold. No, that isn't what we are talking about. Once the Lord has revealed a truth to us, we however, should not ignore it or walk contrary to it, especially if we want to reap the blessings of God.

What about God's promises? We don't walk beneath these promises He has revealed to us. Admittedly, it takes time to walk out each promise. If God delivered us from listening to rock and roll music, smoking, a critical spirit, or anger, why revert back to those things? Neither should we walk beneath the standards we have set for ourselves such as moral living, our skills, and our relationships to others, our relationship to God, and our positive talk. With the help of the Lord, we may have conquered a tendency to condemn the way people dress, drive their car, or discipline their children. Let's not go back to that old self.

One more important point concerning how not to walk. Scripture warns against walking in unbelief. The writer of Hebrews tells us, "Take heed, brethren, lest there be in any of you an evil heart of unbelief, in departing from the living God."(Heb. 3:12) (See also Heb. 4:11) If we however, repent of walking in unbelief, God will restore us. (Acts 3:19)

How are we to walk?

Now for the positive side of walking in the kingdom. We turn to Colossians 2:6 AMP.: "As you have therefore received Christ, [even] Jesus the Lord, [so] walk—**regulate your lives and conduct yourselves —in union with and conformity to Him**" How did you receive Christ? Go back to verse 5 (AMP.): "...in such] orderly array and the firmness *and* the solid front *and* steadfastness of your faith in Christ, [that leaning of the entire human personality on Him in absolute **trust and confidence in His power, wisdom and goodness**]."

Wuest's Expanded translation reads, (v. 5-6), "In the same manner, therefore, as you received Christ Jesus the Lord, **in Him be constantly ordering your behavior,** having been rooted with the present result that you are firmly established,…"

How did we receive Christ? The above verses tell us—by total trust in Him. It wasn't even our faith. It was His faith as a gift to us, otherwise we could boast. "For by grace are ye saved through faith, and that not of yourselves..." (Eph. 2:8-9) From the Greek, taking note of the tenses, the full translation reads: "By grace you have been saved in past time completely, with the result that you are in a state of salvation which persists through present times" (*Word Studies in The Greek New Testament* Vol. 1, p 66 Wuest).

So then how do we walk in Him? By total trust in Jesus Christ. From verse 6, "received" is *paralambano*, to take to, to join to one's self—to personally appropriate to one's self. "Rooted" means that you are firmly anchored. "Stablished" refers to a process going on.

Part of the "walking in Him" is to trust in His direction, in the little and the big decisions of life, even though circumstances and logic would tell us to do the opposite or our own way. We don't follow a philosophy of the world; instead we put our trust in what God says or the Word says. This is walking by faith and not by sight. (2 Cor. 5:7)

We try to walk out where we are now, in the truths that have been revealed to us already, that is, our present reality, not where we are going to be. When we were freshmen in high school we didn't attempt to master senior or college level course work. We simply took one step at a time. This does not however, negate goal setting or working toward visions. Quoting from my book, "*The Rising Son*" page 93: "Concerning the spiritual (growth) in each area of your life, in whatever realm or stage of that realm that you have mastered, be established in that truth, then get ready to move to the next realm."

A few other scriptures on how to walk. "For we are God's [own] handiwork (His workmanship) created in Christ Jesus, [born anew] that we may do those good works which God predestined (planned beforehand) for us **(taking paths which He prepared ahead of time) that we should walk in them**—living the good life which He prearranged and made ready for us to live." (Eph. 2:10 AMP)

Today, through books, tapes, periodicals, videos, newsletters, preaching, and the Internet, we have a wealth of Christian teaching available. Yet with such privileged information come responsibilities. We are to walk consistently. "I therefore, the prisoner of the Lord, beseech you that ye walk worthy of the vocation wherewith ye are called." (Eph. 4:1) To rule and reign with Christ, we must walk consistently on a daily basis, not up one day and down the next.

We are to walk honestly. "Let us walk honestly, as in the day; not in rioting and drunkenness, not in chambering and wantonness, not in strife and envying." (Rom. 13:13) The previous verse states that the day is at hand. We are to walk in wisdom, to behave wisely, especially toward non-believers. "Walk in wisdom toward them that are without, (those on the outside of Christian circles) redeeming the time." (Col. 4:5) NAS: "...making most of the opportunity." We are to walk as the wise. (Eph. 5:15)

Walk in the light

In the gospel of John, Jesus taught the people, "Yet a little while is the light with you. **Walk while ye have the light,** lest the darkness come upon you: for he that walketh in darkness knoweth not whether he goeth. While ye have light, believe the light, that ye may be the children of the light...." (John 12:35-36) "Light" here means spiritual understanding. Jesus is that Light. The phrase "Lest the darkness come upon you" isn't referring to a loss of salvation, and most certainly doesn't refer to being cast into hell. "Darkness" means a lack of the presence of Jesus, ignorance of spiritual things, and being void of spiritual understanding.

If we receive light in a particular area of our life, and the Lord continues to speak to us about it, but we refuse to walk in that light, then darkness will likely overtake us in that area of our life. We may also even lose the spiritual knowledge and understanding that we had to begin with in that part of our life. This doesn't contradict however, what we discuss elsewhere in regard to laying something on the shelf for a time. For example, let's say that the Lord reveals to us that we act prideful in the way we dress. If we refuse to act on that revelation, that is, take steps to correct that attitude, then darkness, or lack of spiritual understanding in regard to our dress may come upon us.

Walking in the Kingdom is a continuous series of walks from darkness to light in each area of our life. "If we say that we have fellowship with him, and walk in darkness, we lie, and do not the truth: But if we walk in the light, as he is in the light, we have fellowship one with another, and the blood of Jesus Christ his Son cleanseth us from all sin." (1 John 1:6-7) In other words, we fellowship with the Father and He with us. Therefore, we need to walk in all the light (spiritual understanding) we have.

"Thy word is a lamp unto my feet, and a light unto my path." (Ps. 119:105) It matters not how spiritual we may appear, if we don't walk by the light of God's Word in each part of our life, we risk stumbling. But when we apply the Word of God as lamp unto our feet or our walk, nothing will be hidden from our (spiritual) eye.

The word "feet" from Strong's means by impl. a step, a foot as used in walking .The word "path" (Strong's #5410) means to tramp; a (beaten) track. Thus we might say that "feet" speaks of our daily walk or activity while "path" refers to our lifestyle and to our future where we might walk. The Word of God will not only keep us from falling or taking a wrong turn in our daily living but it will light our path. The Word or the wisdom of God is not limited. So He places no limits to our spiritual growth or to where we can walk, now or in the future.

Proverbs 10 explains walking in integrity. "He who walks with integrity walks securely, But he who perverts his ways will become known." (Prov. 10:9 NKJV) We need to aggressively work on eliminating the works of flesh in our life, especially once the Lord has shined the light on that part of our life. We can then walk securely. "To speak evil of no man, to be no brawlers, but gentle, showing all meekness unto all men." (Titus 3:2 KJV)

Isaiah describes the path of the righteous in Isaiah 26:7 (AMP): "The way of the [consistently] righteous—those living in religious and moral rectitude in every area and relationship of their lives—is level *and* straight. You O' *Lord*, Who are upright, direct aright *and* level the path of the [uncompromisingly] just *and* righteous." We need to pray daily this prayer from Jeremiah, "(Pray) That the LORD thy God may shew us the way wherein we may walk, and the thing that we may do." (Jer. 42:3)

How do we walk in the will of God? We may think that once we "know" the will of God in our life, that we can take it easy and just follow that path. Penelope Stokes, in *Faith, the Substance of Things Unseen* writes, "But life doesn't work that simply. The reality is, God expects us to choose—not once, but over and over again. The Lord gives us, as we grow, increasing responsibility...and calls us to increasing accountability. And that spectrum that is designated as "the will of God" is not a tiny black bulls-eye on a target, but a vast, broad realm of possibility involving innumerable choices, all of which could be "God's will" for our life."

In Genesis the 32nd chapter, we read where Jacob's name was changed. "So He said to him, "What is your name?" He said, "Jacob." And He said, "Your name shall no longer be called Jacob, but Israel; for you have struggled with God and with men, and have prevailed." (Gen. 32:27-28 NKJV) After the Lord has smitten us, we walk with that familiar limp.

True Israelites in the Old Testament represent the believers today. Their spiritual walk (Gen. 32:31) betrays true Israelites. That is, the Lord has crippled our old desires and our old ways. Through tribulation, we have learned patience. When God hits our thigh or the area of our loins, which represents our natural strength and ability to reproduce, His divine nature then manifests itself. (2 Pet. 1:4)

Referring to the Israelites in the wilderness, "Thy raiment waxed not old upon thee, neither did thy foot swell, these forty years." (Deut. 8:4) "Neither did thy feet swell"- means that they were able to maintain their walk with God toward the promised inheritance. For us today, in our wilderness experiences, or at any time for that matter, if we remain faithful to God, He will see that we maintain our walk with Him toward the promise. The raiment speaks of our covering. God will keep His covering, that is, His protection and guidance, over us without wavering. By covering us, He helps keep us from being deceived.

Now Deuteronomy 8:2, "And thou shalt remember all the way which the LORD thy God led thee these forty years in the wilderness, to humble thee, and to prove thee, to know what was in thine heart, whether thou wouldest keep his commandments, or no." The "way" speaks of our spiritual walk.

Four Walking in the Furnace

The book of Daniel presents to us a valuable lesson on walking in the Kingdom. Shadrach, Meshach and Abed-Nego had been thrown bound into the fiery furnace because they would not bow to the golden image. (Dan. 3:10-12) Dan. 3:16-18 NKJV, "Shadrach, Meshach, and Abed-Nego answered and said to the king, "O Nebuchadnezzar, we have no need to answer you in this matter. If that is the case, our God whom we serve is able to deliver us from the burning fiery furnace, and He will deliver us from your hand, O king. But if not, let it be known to you, O king, that we do not serve your gods, nor will we worship the gold image which you have set up."

"Then these men were bound in their coats, their trousers, their turbans, and their other garments, and were cast into the midst of the burning fiery furnace." (Dan. 3:21 NKJV) Notice that they were bound **before** they went into the furnace. We are often bound in our trials, our tribulations, and our problems even before the Holy Spirit begins to burn in our heart concerning our problem.

Verse 22 tells us that the men who threw the Hebrew men into the fire were slain. So the same fire of the Holy Spirit that cleanses us destroys those of the world. How is that? What do we, the children of God have, that needs to be burned up? Is it not those things of the world that bind us? But the people of the world have nothing going for them but the philosophies and ways of the world, so when that same fire of the Holy Spirit convicts them, it destroys them. We are not talking about death or destruction of their life but destruction of their way of life.

"Nebuchadnezzar spoke to his counsellors, "Look!" he answered, "I see four men **loose, walking** in the midst of the fire; and they are not hurt, and the form of the fourth is like the Son of God." (Dan. 3:25 NKJV) The fire was seven times hotter than normal (or fair). When we feel that we get more problems than we deserve, we think God is unfair in His dealings with us.

Notice two things in this verse. They were loose and they were walking. Even though they were loose, they didn't leap for the exit door of the furnace. They had the power to get out. But instead of trying to get out, they kept on walking. They allowed God to process them until His image was burned in them, until they received the total purification. God today desires to purify the body of Christ.

When most believers see a way out of their trials, they scramble as fast as they can to get out. They shout, "God, get me out of this mess!" Or "the devil has me on the run" or "God, why did you allow this to happen to me." If instead, we would, with God, walk out the trial and problem we are in, and allow Him to finish the processing and the burning off the chaff in that problem in our life until it is finished, we would see victory more often and wouldn't get trapped in the next furnace.

These Hebrew men walked in the midst of the furnace. Notice, however, that they didn't see the fourth man, one like the Son of God. When we are in the midst of our trouble, all we see is the fire and wonder how we can get out. The Hebrew word for "see" in verse 25 means a vision (Strong's #2370), so Nebuchadnezar had a vision of the four in the furnace. People on the outside of our situation can often see God working in us in our problems. While that fire of the Holy Spirit burns away our flesh, that is, our carnal desires, we are blind to seeing God trying to work out something in our life. Rather than deliver us from our problems, God often leads us through our problems, often through a processing. Paul emphasized, "I know how to be abased, and I know how to abound. Everywhere and in all things I have learned both to be full and to be hungry, both to abound and to suffer need." (Phil. 4:12 NKJV)

God does not force His way into your heart. Rather, He wants you to willingly open your heart to Him, both initially and as you progress in your Christian walk. This influence, to work, must supersede your natural desires. Opening your heart to God is saying yes to his processing, just as Mary, (the mother of Jesus) declared, "Be it so unto me according to thy word." (Luke 1:38) It is letting God's Word work in you and trusting Him even when the process gets painful, when you feel the fire of the Holy Spirit burning your flesh. This burning speaks of a cleaning fire of the Holy Spirit that tries you on your road to sonship. But it will not singe one hair of your head (spiritual covering) nor leave the smell of smoke upon you, but it will burn off your bondages and leave you free to walk unharmed in the midst of the fire with one like unto the Son of God. God is not out to punish you but to make you fruitful.

So often, as we go through trials, we cry out to God, "Why did I deserve this?" We deserve afflictions, but afflictions don't come to us because we deserve them. Our life in the Kingdom of God is not determined by either what we deserve or don't deserve but by what God sees we need for our processing.

Elijah Walks out the Word

In the 17th Chapter of 1 Kings we see how Elijah walks out the Word of the Lord. The Lord God had told Elijah to go hide by the brook Cherith. The word "Cherith" means to cut or divide (like a two edged sword). The Word of God is as sharp as a two edged sword, so as we absorb the Word of God, hidden from the world, God will reveal Himself to us and feed us spiritually.

Ravens were to feed him there (v. 4). The Lord declared ravens as unclean birds. I believe however, that these were not literal birds but a group of unclean people in the area who fed him bread and flesh in the morning and evening. God will often use people in our lives we think are unfit (unclean) to serve God, people we think are far below our level of education, our standing in society, our position or our degree of understanding of the Kingdom. But we had better listen to them. We see here another example of the importance of listening to God when we are in need.

"So he went and did according unto the word of the LORD: for he went and dwelt by the brook Cherith, that is before Jordan." (1 Kings 17:5) Now verses 7-9 state, "And it came to pass after a while, that the brook dried up, because there had been no rain in the land. And the word of the LORD came unto him, saying, Arise, get thee to Zarephath, which belongeth to Zidon, and dwell there: behold, I have commanded a widow woman there to sustain thee." Zarephath means smelting furnace; refine; from a word which means to fuse (such as metal).

It was the widow woman, an unlikely source, who would sustain Elijah, but in the process, God would bless her. The point is that Elijah walked through a process, where first he depended upon the ravens for food. Second, his source of water dried up (v. 7), (no fresh Word) and third, he had to depend upon a poor widow. When Elijah got to her, she was indeed not only poor but was planning to eat her last meal because of the apparent famine (no rain). Yet, God sent Elijah to her. It must have been humbling for Elijah, a great man of God, to go to a poor widow for food. Yet, through that process, God restored the widow's supply so that she did not run out.

The widow woman represents the church (without Husband Jesus) struggling to survive. But God is sending a ministry to bring restoration. The meal represents the bread or the Word of God while the oil speaks of the anointing of the Holy Spirit. (John 16:13). It takes the two together to bring life to you. Today a famine has swept the land of hearing the true Word. (Amos 8:11). Elijah, with a word from the Lord assured the woman, "…the barrel of meal shall not waste, neither shall the cruse of oil fail, until the Day that the Lord sendeth rain upon the earth." (v. 14) That "Day" is the 7th day, or the 7th 1000-year day we are now entering (2 Pet. 3:8).

The woman (church) obeyed the Word of God and she did eat. The church, which is now hungry for the deeper Word, we find beginning to obey the Word brought to them. God, through the sons of God, supplies the meal and oil to the church.

Note that Elijah was fed by the ravens (1 Kings 17:6) (30-fold), the woman (17:9) (60-fold), and by the angel (19:6)(100-fold). We, like Elijah, need to accept the Word of God from ministry in the 30, 60 and 100 fold realms.

Now the woman's son was sick until there was no breath left in him. (v. 17) Elijah stretched himself on the lad three times (three is a number of perfection) and cried unto God. "And he stretched himself upon the child three times, and cried unto the LORD, and said, O LORD my God, I pray thee, let this child's soul come into him again. And the LORD heard the voice of Elijah; and the soul of the child came into him again, and he revived." (1 Kings 17:21-22)

Now verse 24 says, "And the woman said to Elijah, Now by this I know that thou art a man of God, and that the word of the LORD in thy mouth is truth." God had changed Elijah's source of supply. In our walk with the Lord, we cannot depend upon any one source except God. Our employer or our mailbox isn't our source. Rather God is our source. Through Elijah's obedience in his walk with the Lord, and the woman' s obedience to the instructions of the man of God, the boy revived. The widow woman also received supplies until the famine ended. When we walk according to the Word of God, then the world will recognize us as the sons of God and that the words we speak are true.

How Fast can We Walk?

This may seem like an unusual question. Whether we're discussing revealed knowledge, correction, spiritual gifts, or deliverance, some Christians can handle more than others can. How fast we walk depends upon how fresh the revelation and upon how it relates to that in which we already walk. For example, if God reveals to us a large number of our faults at one time, some of us will get discouraged. Some of us will get frustrated in trying to correct our faults. It depends on our emotional and spiritual maturity

On the other and, some of us, especially the sons of God, can walk them out rather rapidly. What if God revealed to us all the spiritual knowledge that we received in the past year, all in one day? Could we walk in them? To learn to walk, for some, takes more time than for others. We walk them out one step at a time. We aren't in a sprint race but a marathon. Yet, except what he imposes on himself, there is no limit to how fast a son of God can walk.

You might ask, "Why can the sons of God walk faster than others can?" They receive greater revelations from the Lord. Consider the servant realm, the friend realm and the son realm. "Henceforth I call you not servants; for the servant knoweth not what his lord doeth: but I have called you friends; for all things that I have heard of my Father I have made known unto you." (John 15:15 KJV)

"Wherefore thou art no more a servant, but a son; and if a son, then an heir of God through Christ." (Gal. 4:7) Furthermore, the sons walk faster because they possess and exercise more of the gifts and more effectively demonstrate how God has trained them, for the Spirit leads them. (Rom. 8:14)

We must walk by faith. If we always waited for the perfect conditions or perfect knowledge in our life, we will never take the next step. And often if we don't take that step when we are led, especially in the spiritual realm, we will remain as spiritual babes. We need to advance beyond the milk stage. (1 Cor. 3:2-3; Heb. 5:12-14)

After finishing my Masters degree at the University of Minnesota in 1960, a phone call came to the department where I received my degree. They wanted a teacher in a Junior college in New York and they needed him right away. School had been in session for two weeks. By just one brief phone conversation between the superintendent of the school, and the head of the department where I got my degree, and me, the superintendent said I could have the job. My wife and I only had a few hours to decide whether I should to take the job or not. I decided to accept. We would live in a completely furnished duplex. How could my wife sell all our furniture and appliances in three weeks? We had no time to even think about it. But by the grace of God, she did sell them, mostly within the last two or three days of the three-week period.

I took a flight to the school and began teaching the next day. I had never taught school before. In three weeks I flew back to pick up my wife and daughter. I had far from perfect knowledge for this position. Again, from a personal example, if we wait for perfect conditions or perfect knowledge, we may never take the next step. In this case, I know that I made the right decision, even though I wasn't a born again Christian at the time. Looking back, I was willing to face the unknown for the challenge and excitement of the new. See Chapter 8 for further lessons from this teaching position.

In our Kingdom walk, God may, from time to time, deal with several different attitudes we defend or habits we shield. We may need to walk out anger or we may need to become more tolerant toward certain personalities or we may need to develop a proper attitude about what people do to us. The Lord may have just recently revealed some subtle thing about our attitude. We may have developed this attitude years ago but now the Lord sees the time to deal with it. It may relate to fellow workers, neighbors, church members, family members, or attitudes and prejudices toward people of other races, culture, or personalities, or how people dress, spend their money, discipline their children, or spend their time.

Such an approach doesn't mean we become tolerant of sin. But if God deals with us on such a matter, then we must take the proper steps. If we drive to work every day in heavy traffic, we may develop bad attitudes toward drivers who follow too close, drivers who cut in front of us, or those who don't dim their lights. It's these kinds of attitudes we need to walk out or work on changing.

Some things, whether corrections or revelations, may take a relatively short time to walk out—days or weeks, while others may take months or years. It took my wife three years to walk out the healing of her eyes so that she didn't have to wear glasses. She started to read a big print Bible and kept progressing to smaller print as her eyes improved. She never cheated by wearing glasses or sunglasses. Previously she never went anywhere without her sunglasses. Yet, she determined to walk out the healing of her eyes. At first, when she ministered from the pulpit, it was difficult to refocus on the Bible after speaking forth what the Holy Spirit gave her. She told the people what the Lord was doing, but no one came against her.

Whether they are revelations or corrections, they can come directly from the Lord or through other people. Directions can be learning new skills, natural or spiritual. We must walk them out until they become a part of us, that is, a part of our nature. If it was a habit or a thought pattern that was ungodly, then when we have walked out that correction that habit is no longer a part of us or a part of our nature.

Ordered Behavior

Now back to the meaning of "ordered behavior" as Wuest's Translation expresses the word "walk." To me it means walking with direction, with meaning, and with purpose. As to direction, do we know where we came from? We must neither be a prisoner of nor despise our past. We don't discount our childhood or our salvation experience but we need to continue to move on with God. We can't continue to live on yesterday's anointing, last week's service, last month's revival or last year's convention. Neither do we drive down stakes and set up camp at any step along the way, but again, we move on with God. We follow the cloud by day and the fire by night as the Israelites did. And again, we don't discount these experiences. We recognize how we arrived where we now dwell in God. If we have greatly advanced spiritually, then we give God the glory.

Next, you need to know who you are now and know who you are in the Lord God. As to "direction," we need to know where we are going. Have a vision; see later on vision in the next chapter. But we leave much of our "direction" to Jesus Christ.

The word "meaning" has to do with the way and manner in which we walk. Each "spiritual" step we take should have meaning in our life and have a positive affect on the lives we touch.

As for "purpose" in our walk or ordered behavior, God had a purpose in mind when He created the universe and all its details. God obviously had a purpose for His only Begotten Son (Isa. 61:1-3; Luke 4:18-19)— that He would be the saviour of the world (John 3:16; 4:42) He created man to populate the earth, that man would worship God, would manifest His nature in the earth, and would bring Him glory (Ps. 22:23; John 15:8; Rom. 15:6). God also has a purpose for the (true) Church and it's up to each member in the body of Christ to walk in harmony with that purpose. Each person in the body of Christ is important. Now we, the sons of God, in constant progress toward His image (2 Cor. 3:18), walk with divine purpose.

CHAPTER 6

▼

WHAT FACTORS AFFECT OUR WALK IN THE KINGDOM?

Many aspects of our lives affect our walk in the Kingdom. The following list is not the final word, but should be a good start to better understand the Kingdom walk. Many are interrelated.

1. Our placement or adoption.

2. Our relationship with God.

3. Our degree of commitment; obedience.

4. Our goals and the extent that we set and work toward those goals.

5. Our set of priorities.

6. Our value system.

7. Our nature or the extent of how developed is our God-like nature.

8. Our degree of holiness.

9. Our experiences in life—our natural and emotional maturity.

10. Our spiritual maturity.

1. Our placement or adoption

Our placement or adoption in the Kingdom of God is no doubt the greatest factor that affects our walk in the Kingdom. "But when the fulness of time was come, God sent forth his Son, made of a woman, made under the law, To redeem them that were under the law, that we might receive the adoption of sons." (Gal. 4:4-5)

What do these verses mean? First, it speaks of an appointed time for the incarnation of the Son of God. Second, God sent His Son Jesus, into the world to be born of a woman. Third, these verses show that the great purpose of His coming was that we might be redeemed and receive adoption as a son.

The term "adoption" in the scriptures however, doesn't mean the same as in our modern western culture. According to the Scriptures, a son was adopted when he was 30 years old. In that culture adoption was a public occasion when a son who had proven his responsibility and faithfulness was proclaimed as a son. The son then received certain rights—to use his father's name and to transact business in his father's name. He had the power of attorney and was given his inheritance. That is, he was given equality with his Father.

An infant *(teknion)* (often translated "little child") is one who gets exited about what they receive, such as forgiveness of sins, gifts of the Spirit, healing and blessings. (1 John 2:1) The youth or young men (*teknon*) on the other hand, rejoice in their strength to live as overcomers in the world. (1 John 2:13)

The mature son (*huios*), then and now, knows and walks the way of the Father, filled with the understanding and will of the Father. He has matured spiritually and walks like he has the mind of Christ. The mature son uses his authority and the name of Jesus with discernment and discretion. He doesn't take that authority lightly; neither does he abuse it. The mature, adopted son walks in confidence and assurance of who he is and his source (Jesus) of all things.

The adopted son walks in a leadership role with authority but without arrogance. Yet without such leadership, there is no way the others (the subjects) can walk in the Kingdom, for they continue to grope in darkness.

2. Our Relationship with God

Our relationship with God relates to where we dwell, that is, in the 30, 60 or 100 fold realm (Matt. 13:23), but it is much broader than that. Our walk depends upon how much we walk out what we know. How well we obey the direction we get from God often determines how clearly we hear His further directions. If we keep ignoring the voice of God, we will soon find ourselves in spiritual darkness. We walk in what we believe to be true. Equally true, God doesn't expect us to walk in what we don't know.

We need to examine the quality of our prayer life and the quality of our (personal or group) Bible study. These heavily influence our knowledge of God, which in turn influences our daily walk. We grant God top priority of our time. We aren't speaking of knowing about God, but knowing Him intimately. You get to know someone intimately only by spending quality time with him or her on a continual basis. The same holds true for knowing God.

Philip had asked Jesus to show them the Father. "Jesus saith unto him, Have I been so long time with you, and yet hast thou not known me,

Philip? he that hath seen me hath seen the Father; and how sayest thou then, Show us the Father? Believest thou not that I am in the Father, and the Father in me? the words that I speak unto you I speak not of myself: but the Father that dwelleth in me, he doeth the works." (John 14:9-19)

Because the Father dwelt in fullness in Christ, whoever had seen Christ had seen the Father. They saw not his physical features, but the nature and character of God the Father. When Christ lives in fullness in any believer, ordering and controlling their conduct and life, then whoever looks upon that person has also seen the Christ.

When we allow the Christ to manifest His nature and character in us and through us, people begin to see the Christ in us. We do not struggle to be holy, pure, or righteous but allow Christ whom is holy, pure and righteous to live and abide within us. Our relationship to people or the things around us counts much less than our intimate relationship to Christ. These others will take care of themselves.

3. Our Degree of Commitment.

To what extent do we totally commit our lives to God? To what extent do we commit ourselves and follow through, to others, to our word, to the projects we start, and to holiness. Consider Romans 12:11 (Wuest's translation), "With respect to zeal, not lazy", not slothful in business—committed to do well in the tasks or jobs we do. These traits heavily influence our walk and how we progress in the Kingdom. We will cross through valleys of darkness, climb mountains, overcome troubles, fight battles, yet not without both physical and spiritual battle fatigue.

A Christian who has grown up spiritually wasn't raised in a hot house. Neither do they find their path of life all on lush carpet. One of the secrets to a victorious Kingdom walk is to not look down at our feet and individual steps (circumstances). When we look down, our walk becomes legalistic and ritualistic. Instead, we look up to the spiritual realm, to

Jesus Christ, following the vision—focusing instead on the Word and the promises of God. Abraham staggered not at the promise of God. Rom. 4:20, "He staggered not at the promise of God through unbelief; but was strong in faith, giving glory to God;"

Walking successfully in this Kingdom comes by tribulation and crucifying the old nature. Yet some believers don't like to hear about tribulation, suffering, sacrifice or self-discipline. The Kingdom walk isn't always easy. It's not a Sunday afternoon stroll in the park. "Confirming the souls of the disciples, and exhorting them to continue in the faith, and that we must through much tribulation enter into the kingdom of God." (Acts 14:22) I believe that most believers battle more against the flesh than they do the forces on the outside.

It's not enough to simply accumulate knowledge of the Lord or to receive revelation of the Scriptures. Before such knowledge brings results, we need to walk it out in our every day life. I can read all kinds of books on gardening but until I apply that knowledge by planting seed, watering and weeding the garden, I can't reap any harvest. God told Abraham that he could have the land that he could see. But He told Joshua that every place that the sole of his foot would tread was his. We have to walk out our revelations we receive.

The Lord spoke to Jeremiah, "But this is what I commanded them, saying, obey my voice: and I will be your God, and you will be my people, and you will walk in all the way which I command you; that it may be well with you. Yet they did not obey or incline their ear, but walked in their own counsel and in the stubbornness (KJV: imagination) of their evil heart and went backward and not forward." (Jer. 7:23-24 NAS)

The Kingdom walk develops as we allow the Holy Spirit to have full control of our lives. **This is obedience.** If we desire to walk in the Kingdom, we must accept the discipline of the Holy Spirit. The Kingdom won't come to the disobedient. 1 Pet. 1:14-15 exhorts us, "(Live)...As obedient children, not fashioning yourselves according to the former lusts in your ignorance: But as he which hath called you is holy, so be ye holy in all manner of conversation;" The NKJV: "…you also be holy in all your conduct." Isaiah declared, "If ye be willing and obedient, ye shall eat the good of the land:" (Isa. 1:19) The land speaks of our body or our life. If we are obedient, we will reap blessings in our life.

Let us quote from Brother Bill Britton's book, *The Kingdom in Action*, another excellent book for anyone who wants to grow in the Kingdom walk. "This kingdom must not only be preached and entered, but it must also be lived, **be manifested to the world through the lives of his saints.** Some people seem to think that since they now have a higher revelation of the Word, that they don't have to live as holy as they did when they were under legalistic preaching. How wrong they are. This kingdom message and kingdom life brings a walk of holiness and purity that is as natural to the saints as breathing. There is no effort to producing righteousness when you have entered and are walking in the kingdom realm. It is your life".

Speaking of Titus 2:11, Brother Britton continues, "So grace does not teach us that we can follow after the desires of the old man, or satisfy the craving of Adam's evil nature. Real grace teaches us to deny ungodliness and worldly lusts." Kingdom walking is a fervent desire, a commitment to do good, to live holy, and to deny that which is evil.

We must commit ourselves to grow up spiritually in God, despite the rough terrain. The enemy is not going to lie down and play dead when you make a quality decision to follow hard after God. James exhorts us, "Submit yourselves therefore to God. Resist the devil, and he will flee from you." (Jas. 4:7) We often forget the first part of this verse: "Submit to God."

We can no longer fear to move on, because the nature of life is rooted in many different experiences, in many trials as well as mountain-top experiences. We needed each previous realm and each previous trial to accomplish its purpose in us. **But we need to continue to purpose to walk in a new day or new expression of Jesus Christ manifesting Himself in us and through us.** A step in the Kingdom in itself implies a step forward, a step which allows the Christ within us to manifest Himself. In each of these steps we gain spiritual growth.

We need to make a determined effort toward the goal of moving on with God—it will not occur if we lead a passive life. Our walk will continually change as we move on and at times it will take adjustment on our part to each new step or gait. But it is "God which worketh in you both to will and to do of His good pleasure." (Phil. 2:13) And it is the Holy Spirit within us who gives us the power to walk that walk. Not only that, but God gives us the desire, (will) to walk that walk. The Greek in this verse indicates that this is a process of God working His thoughts in our lives to cause a change in our outward manifestation.

Paul wrote: "I am crucified with Christ." We would like the Lord to take care of that inner working of the cross in one big moment. "And he (Jesus) said to them all, If any man will come after me, let him deny himself, and take up his cross daily, and follow me." (Luke 9:23) Notice, this is a daily, on-going process. Without a deep sense of commitment, we tend to reject the daily grind of the cross, that chastening and processing in which God takes us through. We readily go to the cross for forgiveness of sin, but can we go to the cross daily to accept the crucified life? So many times we expect to enjoy the privileges of the cross, but refuse it's demands. To follow Jesus to the cross means we are willing to die to our old self. What does it mean to take up our cross daily and follow Jesus? Our cross is the thing that bothers us the most.

Jesus, as He hung on the cross, cried "It is finished." We must believe in our heart, if we are truly born again, that Jesus has taken care of all our past sins. He is also faithful and just to forgive us our sins, if we will but confess them. (1 John 1:9) But to really know the reality of the resurrection, we must firmly believe He has not only taken care of our past sins, but has removed all sense of guilt.

Concerning the gathering of the manna, we read in Exodus 16:16-18 (NKJV), "This is the thing which the LORD has commanded: 'Let every man gather it according to each one's need, one omer for each person, according to the number of persons; let every man take for those who are in his tent.'" Then the children of Israel did so and gathered, some more, some less. So when they measured it by omers, he who gathered much had nothing left over, and he who gathered little had no lack. Every man had gathered according to each one's need."

The account of the manna teaches us many spiritual lessons. The Israelites ate the manna for natural energy. Manna symbolizes the Word of God. We must gather, consume, and digest the Word of God daily, rather than store it away in our mind. That is, we must walk it out daily in our lives. Each person is to work out (walk out) their own salvation with fear and trembling. (Phil. 2:12)

Notice also that each man had to gather for his own tent or household. (Our body or total being is our household). Each man was responsible to gather no more, no less than the family's daily needs. Applying that principle today, some people get more, some people get less spiritual wisdom from a given church service, passage of Scripture or Christian literature. We walk out not just the Scriptures but all of what God reveals to us. Each of us become responsible to "clean the wax out of our spiritual ear" and hear the Word of God for ourselves and then act responsibly for what we hear—obey the Word as the Holy Spirit leads. Some of this wisdom and truth will come direct from the Scriptures, but some will come from the leadership ministry, that is, the five-fold ministry and other leaders of the local church, the sons of God, and other leaders in the Body of Christ. It is this ministry who hears the most from God, for that is God's order. (Amos 3:7)

The lesson is this: each of us must commit to walk our own walk; we must personally obey leading and direction that God reveals to us. No one else can walk it out for us. Yes, we do get strength and help directly from God and from the rest of the body (for we are to share one another's burdens), but the final responsibility lies with us. In reality, we don't walk in our own strength but in His as we yield to Him.

Each of us must commit to **hear** God for ourselves. In reality it's us hearing ourselves speak the Word of God. (Rom. 10:17). In Luke 6:17-19 it speaks of the multitude…which came to **hear** him (Jesus) and to be healed of their diseases. In Matthew chapter 5, Jesus told the woman with the issue of blood, "...Daughter, thy faith hath made thee whole; go in peace and be whole of thy plague" (v.34). Then Matthew 14 states that when the people had knowledge of Jesus, they brought the sick unto Him and He healed them. How did they have that knowledge of Jesus? By **hearing** something about Him. How did the woman with the issue of blood get faith? She **heard** about Jesus. Each of those people that heard about the healing anointing of Jesus then committed themselves to act on what they had heard.

My wife and I, as a team, walk some things out together. For example, major financial matters we discuss before making a decision. Some things, however, I have to walk out alone. In some cases our local church has to walk out many things together. It may be church finances or other special projects, or it may be the problems of an individual member or family. The rest of the church members get behind them in prayer, finances, encouragement, commitment or whatever other help it takes. .

The Old Testament illustrates this same principle describing the journey of the Israelites out of Egypt, "...and there was not one feeble person among their tribes." (Ps. 105:37) This shows that each one walked his own walk; no one had to be carried and it also demonstrates the power of God in keeping them in divine health.

Other accounts in the Old Testament illustrate that responsibility of especially leaders to walk out their calling. For example, David had to walk out his calling to be king. Despite the injustice done to him and the hatred by King Saul who tried to kill him, David committed himself to become king under God's timetable and under God's order rather than use the opportunity to kill Saul. (1 Sam. 24:6; 26:8-11)

Noah committed himself for some 100 years to build an ark and to preach repentance and righteousness because of the Lord's instructions. It was not a weekend project. Many believers today step out in faith and begin to build in response to a vision the Lord has given them, but if they don't see immediate results, get discouraged. Can you imagine the opposition Noah endured? (2 Pet. 2:5; Gen. 6:14-7:24) For commitment and persistent faith, Noah gets an A plus. Likewise, by faith and through continuous commitment, Abraham traveled into the land that God had called him. (Heb. 11:8-11) We read verse 8, "By faith Abraham, when he was called to go out into a place which he should after receive for an inheritance, obeyed; and he went out, not knowing whither he went."

Jacob committed himself to receive Rachel as his wife, working for Laban for 20 years. His son Joseph committed himself to serve God, to become the best prisoner in the entire land of Egypt and God richly rewarded him for his faithfulness. In the New Testament we note how Paul, despite severe persecution, committed himself, in four major missionary journeys, to preach the gospel to the Gentiles.

We must first commit ourselves to God. If we truly love the Lord with all our heart and mind, it really takes no effort to commit ourselves to serve Him, even without bitterness or resentment. We simply do it, for it's part of our nature. We must commit ourselves to study our Bible, even when we don't feel like it. This is discipline. If necessary, we need to ask God to force-feed us.

Some have counted the cost and yet march forward in their commitment to reach for the prize of the high calling in Christ Jesus. Others, after counting the cost, allow fear to hinder their move to a higher realm in their Christian walk. (Luke 14:28)

Concerning the quality of commitment, do we keep our word? If we tell someone or the Lord that we're going to do something, we better see that it gets done, and in the time we say we'll do it! If we say we'll be somewhere by 7 p.m., we better try our best to get there by 7 p.m.

We also must commit ourselves to one another. That is, we must realize that we're not independent beings, each walking in the sphere of our own little kingdom. We need to submit to one another and to the ministries God places in our midst. We are members one of another, bone of His bone, and flesh of His flesh. Yet submitting to one another requires that we become vulnerable to each other. Unfortunately, many hate to do that.

When we open up to others in the body of Christ, we often, as a result, open ourselves up to godly criticism or correction, which is difficult for some. Learning to walk in harmony is not easy.

Those who harden their heart against the Holy Spirit or shut their mind off from Jesus Christ, for whatever reason, become barren like a closed womb. A closed womb can neither receive seed nor can it bring forth any life. Others in the body of Christ bear no fruit because they refuse to grow in God. Some believers shut themselves off because they say, "I don't need any man to teach me." (1 John 1:27) That scripture really means we are to have no natural man or natural mind teach us. We can hear God speak either directly through men or through an anointed man. We can hear from God through the words, actions, and writings of others that hear from God. God not only speaks to us through reading or listening but often when we least expect Him to speak to us, in the midst of life's experiences. He also speaks to us through His lowest messengers, the feet company. If our only source of hearing from God is "the still small voice," then we are in trouble. If we occasionally hear, with discernment, a word contrary to the Scriptures, we can simply reject it. It's like spitting out watermelon seeds.

I have known some believers who fear so much that they may hear wrong doctrine or teaching, that they shut themselves off from the entire rest of the body of Christ! Sadly, they are actually much more likely to hear such false teaching from their own carnal mind. (2 Pet. 2:18)

We read in the book of Numbers the account where the Lord spoke to Moses about the making and use of the silver trumpets. "And the LORD spake unto Moses, saying, Make thee two trumpets of silver; of a whole piece shalt thou make them: that thou mayest use them for the calling of the assembly, and for the journeying of the camps." (Num. 10:1-2)

The verses that follow that portion of Scripture continue to explain the six uses of the trumpets. (1) to call the assembly, (2) journeys, (3) to call the princes, (4) to sound alarms, (5) to go to war, and (6) to announce the feasts (v. 10). Notice that the first purpose of the trumpet is a calling of the assembly. In other words, the number one priority of a Christian is to go to church. The New Testament instructs s us to forsake not the assembling together. I know that some try to explain away that verse.

Some say that going to church Sunday morning is old order, a carry-over ritual from centuries ago. We agree that it isn't the system or organization or our name on the church roll that saves us. It is faith in the person of Jesus Christ who alone saves. On the other hand, we shouldn't go to church every Sunday just to be seen or because it's the thing to do. We go to worship the Lord God, to bless others, to gain spiritual strength from the others, and to give of our (spiritual) strength to them. Some might say they could worship God at home or out on the lake in a boat. The trouble is, they don't worship God like they would in church. I just go by what the Bible says.

I would like to relate a personal testimony. For about seven and one half years I worked the third shift in Tulsa, Oklahoma from 11 p.m. until 7 a.m., plus a 45-minute drive each way from home. Most of that time I worked Saturday nights. Yet in those seven and one half years, I did not miss one single Sunday morning (two hour) service. Usually I only had a one-hour nap before I had to get ready for church. A few times I got an hour and a half, sometimes just a half-hour of sleep and sometimes no sleep at all before church time. But by the grace of God, I didn't miss one church service. The Lord also kept me healthy during that time. I give God the glory that I didn't miss a single day of work due to sickness or bad weather those seven and one half years. Sometime after that when I changed to the day shift, I did require surgery, so then I did miss a few weeks of work. Yet I still did not miss church. In fact, I went to church about three days after my surgery.

Some might excuse themselves from going to church on a given Sunday or even weeknight service, saying, "I didn't feel led of the spirit to go." To them I would ask, "Do you feel led by the spirit to sit down to three meals a day or to go to work each day, or to brush your teeth, or wash the dishes or clean the house?" The eye cannot say to the hand, "I have no need of you."

I can't say to the rest of the body of Christ, "I don't need you. I don't understand your walk; therefore I can't (really saying I won't) walk with you."

We can't walk into the land on our own. It takes the Lord and the rest of the body of Christ to help and guide us. The Lord promised in Exodus, "And I will bring you in unto the land, concerning the which I did swear to give it to Abraham, to Isaac, and to Jacob; and I will give it you for an heritage: I am the LORD." (Exod. 6:8) The "land" represents to us the more fullness of the Kingdom. From Isa. 35:9, "No lion shall be there, nor any ravenous beast shall go up thereon, it shall not be found there; but the redeemed shall walk there:" As we walk on the highway of life and as we commit ourselves to walk worthy on the highway of the Kingdom, the Lord will protect us.

We, that is, the body of Christ, are a house God has formed for Himself. (John 14:2) We must walk worthy. "That ye might walk worthy of the Lord unto all pleasing, being fruitful in every good work, and increasing in the knowledge of God." (Col. 1:10) We need to walk with long suffering and patience, allowing God to perfect us.

The Psalmist gives us sound advice in the following portion of scripture: "Delight thyself also in the LORD; and he shall give thee the desires of thine heart. Commit thy way unto the LORD; trust also in him; and he shall bring it to pass." (Ps. 37:4-5) This doesn't say that He will give us anything we want. The word "way" here means our daily conduct, including our attitudes. This speaks of the desires of our heart, not the object of our desires or the desires of our carnal mind. It doesn't refer to material possessions or even the desires for such things. It states the Lord will put proper, godly desires within our heart, such as a desire to serve Him. The serving itself will come later.

Closely related to commitment is **accountability**. We must not only account for our conduct and our walk with God but also be accountable to our spouse, our family, our job and the rest of the body of Christ. That is, we must be held accountable or responsible for our actions. In today's liberal climate, instead of taking the blame for our own actions, we blame others, society, poverty and a host of other things. In about the last ten years, the word "responsible" has taken on a negative meaning. It's past time to become responsible.

Children need to be held accountable for their actions so that they can learn to be accountable to their employer, their spouse and to God. The "let them do their own thing" mentality of past decades has resulted in a society today where too many people do what they want to do in spite of God's teachings. Our current society, for the most part, has no moral absolutes, and consists of many that jump from job to job, or from marriage to marriage. The Kingdom walk is about accountability. We accept the responsibility for our sins, yet recognize the Christ who forgives.

4. Our Goals.

The apostle Paul, in his own life, set the goal of the prize of the high calling in Christ Jesus. He likewise set missionary goals in his quest to take the gospel to the Gentiles. The goals we set for ourselves must be achievable and realistic. We then cut them into segments so that they do not overwhelm us. We then walk toward those goals where we set new ones. As we plan, with the help and guidance of the Lord, our projects, daily activities and ministries, we set our own deadlines.

Walking toward goals doesn't mean that God dangles the proverbial (spiritual) carrot in front of us, causing us to continually strive, but never reaching our goal. Rather, by the grace of God, we do reach goals that satisfy our spirit. Then if we truly seek the face of God, neither will He allow us to become complacent at each intermediate goal or at each level of our growth or walk. Instead, He will challenge us, open up new goals and new areas of understanding and areas of our own life in which we can mature.

We largely determine **what** we walk in—by what we think or ask. (See Eph. 3:16-19) Verse 20 goes on to say, "Now unto him that is able to do (AMP: "carry out His purpose") exceeding abundantly above all that we ask or think (Concordant Literal N.T.:" requesting or apprehending"), according to the power that worketh in us." It is the Lord Jesus Christ who gives us the things above all that we ask. Verse 20 in the Wuest translation, "...in the measure of the power which is operative in us." Phillips' translation reads: "Now to Him who by his power within us is able to do infinitely more than we even dare to ask or imagine."

Two important points here. First, that same power *(dunamis)* that raised Jesus from the dead works or actively operates within us. That power grants us the ability, to supernaturally, in a measure beyond what we ask or think, **to walk out** what we presently know we should do on a daily basis.

Second, relative to goals, that same power grants us the ability to spiritually see, **to walk toward and to enter into spiritual dimensions** far above and beyond what we could imagine. The power of the Holy Spirit working in our lives is limited only by our willingness to yield to Him. Thus **we** determine **what** God can do for us or **what** we walk in. We almost always live below our potential. We need to enlarge our vision of where we can walk.

Let us not be satisfied to walk in a level lower than that which God has made it possible for us to walk. We should strive not only to live the best we know how and are capable of doing, but strive to move on to greater heights in God. We don't reject but embrace the helps, gifts and weapons that God has provided to help us walk this walk and fight the good fight. Our weapons are not carnal but mighty through God. (2 Cor. 10:4; Eph. 11-17)

In the past many in the charismatic movement were taught to speak to that mountain (trouble), believe, then sit around and wait for God to act. But a key principle was overlooked. After we speak to that mountain and believe, instead of being passive, we need to **start walking toward that mountain.** The real key is to obey what God is dealing with us at the time. In other words, begin to walk and place those problems under our feet; begin to walk in victory over those problems.

One of our higher goals is to ascend into the Lord Jesus Christ. Yet the body will never become the Head. The term "walking" assumes a continuous progress toward a goal, toward some point or toward an intermediate area.

Another high goal is to become the greatest in the Kingdom of God. We desire to achieve this not for self glory, self gratification or a desire to rule over people—But by following the path laid out by Jesus, to become as a child or child like. "Whosoever therefore shall humble himself as this little child, the same is greatest in the kingdom of heaven." (Matt. 18:4). Yet another worthy goal is to be conformed to the image of Jesus Christ, to grow from glory to glory.

One very worthy goal of any believer is to develop the spiritual gifts that lie within us to edify the local body. (1 Cor. 12:1-11) All the spiritual gifts reside within each believer. Then how do we recognize and develop these gifts? We seek God's guidance and the guidance of the leaders in the local church. Attend a church where the gifts are practiced, and study the scriptures and other books concerning the gifts. We must not forget the gift of helps. "And God hath set some in the church, first apostles, secondarily prophets, thirdly teachers, after that miracles, then gifts of healings, helps, governments, diversities of tongues." (1 Cor. 12:28)

Likewise, we need to set goals for our local assembly, for regional churches, for the nation and for the body of Christ worldwide. Jesus set one goal for us: to be witnesses unto Him in Jerusalem (local church), in Judea (area churches or area around us), in Samaria (regionally) and unto the uttermost part of the earth. (Acts 1:8).

Our goal in our local church might include to strengthen our current missionary outreach, to help others by caring, praying, cutting the grass for the widows and elderly, encouraging others, giving people a ride to church or to the grocery store, cooking and other various gifts of helps.

We don't wait for a crisis to set a goal to get us out of a crisis. That's not really proper goal setting. For example, in the area of finances, we can't wait until we are in a financial bind to set a goal to get out of debt. For many, if they would budget their money properly, they wouldn't be so likely to get in that bind. On major financial matters, the husband and wife should discuss things over. In other words, if we don't pray and plan, we'll end up spending our time in crisis management.

It's not enough just to set goals; we need to begin to walk toward those goals. We need to take that step to move out and on with God. Too many Christians sit around and "wait" for God to do something or tell them something. Peter and the other disciples went out in the boat and Jesus came to them walking on the water. Notice that Jesus did not say, "Come" until **after** Peter had said, "**Bid me come.**" "Lord, if it be thou, bid me come unto thee on the water" (Matt. 14:28-29) We need to ask God for the Word, then take that step when we hear it. **Peter made things happen,** while the other disciples, like so many Christians, simply **watch things happen.** Could we paraphrase similar sayings: a third group of people, like those on the land, simply ask, "**What happened?**"

Closely aligned with goals is to have a vision—for yourself, for your place in the body of Christ, and your advancement in the Kingdom of God. Proverbs. 29:18 says, "Where there is no vision, the people perish: but he that keepeth the law, happy is he." Proverbs 29:18 from the NKJV states, "Where there is no revelation, the people cast off restraint;..." A valid vision comes by divine revelation. To cast off restraint means to throw away all order and guidance. Therefore without a divine plan or revelation people will run helter-skelter from church to church, and from doctrine to doctrine without plan or purpose. A vision also speaks of God's divine plan—one of life and immortality.

We need a vision for ourselves, but also very important, beyond ourselves we need a vision for our local church, our community, for the rest of the body of Christ and the nation. We need a vision beyond divine healing and divine health to divine life and immortality—a vision beyond paying tithes and giving tithes to becoming a tithe—a vision beyond the milk and bread of the word to the meat of the word—a vision beyond the elements of the 30 and 60 fold realms to the character of the 100-fold realm.

Let us speak of one more thing about goals. We may have a most worthy goal that we have thought about and worked toward. But God, in His infinite wisdom tells us, "Sorry, but you can't have that goal." What is our reaction? Do we give up or become bitter? Let us learn from David's example.

David had set a goal to build a house for God, but God said no. (1 Chron. 17:4) What did David do? He went to the Lord in prayer and thanksgiving. (2 Sam. 7:18-29) He gave all he had with all his might to the building of the temple—all manner of gold, silver, wood, and precious stones. (1 Chron. 29:2-5) We should give all we have, our very life to the service of the Lord, no matter what may happen to our personal goals, even though worthy, or what people think.

We may need to give of ourselves toward someone else's goals, even future generations, that they would receive the joy and rewards. Someone else may take over the projects or ministry that we have started and worked hard for, but they may end up getting the rewards and possibly the glory. In this light we do any thing God tells us to do and not care who gets the glory. David put much of those precious stones and wealth into the temple but it was never called "David's Temple" but "Solomon's Temple". David didn't get the privilege to rule and reign from that temple or even see it built. Many the saints of old saw the promise (goals) "…did not receive the fulfillment of what was promised." (Heb. 11:39 AMP.)

At best, we try to walk out steps of obedience, one step at a time, where we are now, not where we're going to be. This doesn't, however, do away with or negate goal setting and visions.

Jesus didn't present the Kingdom of God as a Utopia, some far off goal, and one impossible to reach. He declared that the Kingdom of God is within us, is at hand and can now be realized. Since we have the mind of God, if we are the sons of God, He doesn't limit what we can attain. As we advance in the Kingdom of God, such limitations will come to an end. What can we do? Simply change our focus from what we don't have to what we do have.

5. Our Priorities.

Spiritually, we should give priority first to God, then our family, our church, and then our jobs. If in right order, our spirit rules over our soul (mind, will and emotions) and our body. Obviously, we give priority to activities, attitudes and thought patterns that help us to grow spiritually over things that merely satisfy the flesh. For example, if you do have a TV in your home and have the option of watching a secular program or a Christian teaching program, the choice is obvious. Any time that our priorities aren't in order, we will falter in our walk.

In the routine of everyday life—how do we spend our time, our money and our talents? "Moreover, it is required in stewards, that a man be found faithful." (1 Cor. 4:2). Do we keep our bills paid? Do we tithe on a regular basis? ....(Matt. 25:14-15).

6. Our Value System.

Our value system is what we consider important, both tangible and intangible, in our life. What do we value and how do they compare to the other things in our life? The monetary value we place on things is but a fraction of what we refer to as value. For example, what relative value do we place on pleasing and moving on with God, on a peaceful home life, on educating our children or ourselves, (not necessarily formal education), on a successful job for us or our spouse, on having close friends, on the value of our leisure time, on obtaining proper nutrition, on devoting time to a good exercise program? What value do we place on having a quality prayer life, on fellowship with believers, on walking in the Spirit? Or on the negative side, what relative value do we place on pleasing our flesh versus pleasing God or others; of watching sports or soap operas on TV? The list is endless.

Our relative value of things will change over time and thus influence our walk. When we grow older, we give up touch football and bike riding. How much we cling to the past—good or bad—as we grow in the Lord, determines how much these values change as we mature in age or in our spirit. God doesn't let us get by with what we did last year or even two months ago. He has not only changed our desires and our walk, but has convicted us of things that don't please Him. He continues to fine-tune us so that the path we walk gets narrower, for narrow is the way. Some of these things that He asks us to give up may not necessarily be sinful but they are things that weigh us down.

Our values in turn are influenced by the family life in which we grew up and the values our parents had or taught us. Parents have far more influence in instilling values in their children than any other factor. What values did our parents place on us doing well in school? Did they take an interest in our studies and whom we played with as a child? Was there discipline in our home? Was there love? Reverence of God? Regular church attendance? Did they teach us honesty and a healthy work ethic? Did our family get along well or was there continuous strife? Did our parents manage their finances well and teach us how to manage our money? Did our parents live a godly life? The values of right and wrong are taught and learned best in a loving, caring family.

Some people, believers and non-believers alike, determine to overcome certain handicaps and not let the same thing happen to them that happened to their parents. For example, some from broken homes determine to work extra hard in their own marriage to make it successful. Others may determine to get a higher formal education or a higher type of job than of their parents.

As a personal example, my parents and those, especially on my father's side of the family, placed a rather high value on formal education, on honesty, on a close family relationship, both within our immediate family and between families.

All 24 of the grandchildren of my grandparents on my father's side earned a college degree, some with Masters and PhD degrees. Of the next generation, that is, the great grandchildren of my grandparents, the vast majority is college educated, including the girls. Many of them have higher degrees, and most with outstanding jobs and careers. My parents placed a high value on speaking proper grammar, on discipline and teaching self-discipline, on treating all the children equally, on having close friends, on getting along with people. My parents placed a high value on work ethic. I was raised on a dairy and hog farm in Wisconsin and started to milk cows and carried out regular chores when I was just five years old.

You may say, "I was born anew when I was 20 (or 30) years of age. I am a new creature in Christ Jesus and all my past is behind me." Yes, that is true, but it still can influence your value system and thus your walk. Our soul is still in the process of being saved. (Rom. 12:2) In balance, if we have been walking a quality life for the Lord for say, 15 or more years, our past has less and less relevance.

The value system of dedicated Christians differs radically from the value system held by people in the secular world. In the Kingdom walk we simply don't tackle problems like the world does, for the weapons of our warfare are not carnal. For example, Gideon's army, from the Old Testament, defeated their enemy with only 300 men with the help and direction of the Lord.

7. Our nature.

When we accepted Jesus Christ as our Saviour, we received a new nature, a divine nature (2 Pet. 1:4). That divine nature resides within us but it isn't yet fully developed or manifested. It begins with a seed. (John 12:24) At our new birth we begin to walk according to that new nature. We aren't going to change our walk overnight for it is a process, nor will we change it by our own strength and willpower. We may try to walk in this nature in our own strength and even succeed for a while, but we will fall back into our old pattern of bad habits and ungodly attitudes. If we are to change the quality of our walk, we must rely on the power of the Holy Spirit.

When we use our prayer language, we edify ourselves as well as the body of Christ. That Holy Spirit provides that one important source of power.

That new nature must become the dominant force in our walk. The Word of God is food for our spirit, so as we feed our spirit with the Word, we strengthen that new nature so that it becomes the dominant force in our life. In particular areas of our life however, we haven't yet incorporated that new nature.

For example, the Lord may speak to us that we need to praise Him more. We agree and desire to please Him and attempt to walk that out. First of all, that nature of praise must be elevated and stirred up in our **spirit**. Otherwise we will be just praising God from our flesh and our praise walk will end up like a yo-yo, up and down. We have to make up our mind however, that we have to **do something** to walk it out. We do need to rely on the Lord for strength and guidance, yet we can't just sit and expect the Lord to walk it out for us.

An example of how God transformed one man's nature in the Old Testament was the story of Jacob. We notice in Genesis, Chapter 27 how Jacob had deceived his father Isaac into thinking he was Esau. Then in Gen. 27:36 (NKJV) we read, "And Esau said, "Is he not rightly named Jacob? For he has supplanted me these two times. He took away my birthright, and now look, he has taken away my blessing!" He continued, "Have you not reserved a blessing for me?"

In Genesis, Chapter 32 we read the account of Jacob wrestling with the Man (God, v. 28 or Angel, Hos. 12:4-5), "...and the socket of Jacob's hip was out of joint as he wrestled with him" (Gen. 32:25 NKJV). Now verse 28: "And He (the Man) said, 'Your name shall no longer be called Jacob but Israel.'"

God transformed Jacob, the supplanter (schemer or deceiver), into Israel, the prince of God. Jacob was changed in the area of his loins, the area of reproduction (seed or new life). He would no longer reproduce from the natural but from the spiritual. His walk was changed—a walk no longer dominated by his deceitful nature but as a nature of a prince of God. His last son Benjamin was conceived from this changed spiritual nature. That is, Benjamin was born of pure Israel. The loins of our mind speak of the area of new life. Thus, we wrestle with God during the process that changes our nature—which is in the loins of our mind.

8. Our Degree of Holiness.

The extent that we commit ourselves to live a holy life and persist in spending quality time with God will determine the quality of our Christian walk. Holiness stems from a pure attitude not encumbered by rules and regulations. But if our attitude and heart are pure, we will walk in holiness. Holiness is not how we dress or wear our hair, but if our heart is right, we will not only dress right, but also talk and act decently. We will avoid ungodly slang and we will shun gossip, either to listen to or to speak. We will embrace holy teaching. will reverence the things of God and show respect where respect is due.

We can't stop ungodly thoughts from entering our mind but we can stop them from lingering. We will shun the false teaching that "my flesh is not really me, so it can do anything it wants to." And above all, we will walk in love with our fellow man. Kingdom walk is more than talk but involves a purity of our daily conduct and speech. The Kingdom of God is a life to live. "For the kingdom of God is not in word, but in power." (1 Cor. 4:20) Wuest's Expanded, "For the kingdom of God is not in the sphere of speech but in that of power."

Walking in holiness involves bringing our body and mind into subjection to our spirit. Many people, including Christians literally kill themselves by their over-indulgences in soda pop, sweets, junk food, white flour products and in some cases, cigarettes, yet they know better.

"Therefore, to him who knows to do good and does not do it, to him it is sin." (Jas. 4:17 NKJV).

9. Our Life Experiences.

Whether young, middle aged or old, what has taken place in our natural life, that is, the environment in which we were raised or lived, and our spiritual life, will influence our walk. For example, if we were raised in the inner city, the way of life there has a tremendous influence on how we view circumstances, people and even God Himself. If we were raised in a family, which regularly attended church, prayed together and expected God to answer, our walk may be quite different than if our family background related little to the spiritual side of life.

These experiences in turn influence how we think about God and spiritual matters. Yet no matter what our life experiences or and the level of our understanding of spiritual things, we are admonished to be changed by the renewing of our mind. (Rom. 12:2) Sometimes practical knowledge or experiences hinder what God wants us to do. These must be overcome. God does not move by logic but by His Spirit.

10. Our Spiritual Maturity.

How do we acquire spiritual maturity? For one thing, by putting away childish things. We will look at several scriptures concerning spiritual maturity and spiritual growth. "When I was a child, I spake as a child, I understood as a child, I thought as a child: but when I became a man, I put away childish things." (1 Cor. 13:11)

We must strive or follow after Christ, resulting in a straight, stronger walk, and a walk of higher order. Isaiah declared, "For the Lord GOD will help me; therefore shall I not be confounded: therefore have I set my face like a flint, and I know that I shall not be ashamed." (Isa. 50:7) Jesus determined to go to the cross. "And he went a little farther, and fell on his face, and prayed, saying, O my Father, if it be possible, let this cup pass from me: nevertheless not as I will, but as thou wilt." (Matt. 26:39)

"Until we all attain to the unity of the Faith and of the experiential, full, and precise knowledge of the Son of God, to a spiritually mature man, to the measure of the stature of the fulness of the Christ, in that we no longer may be immature ones, tossed to and fro carried around in circles by every wind of teaching in the cunning adroitness of men, in craftiness which furthers the scheming deceitful art of error, but speaking the truth in love, may grow up in Him in all things, who is the Head, Christ" (Eph. 4:13-15 West Expanded).

Another mark of a spiritual mature person is that they practice the principles of the Christian faith and desire the strong meat of the Word, that is, the deeper truths. "But strong meat belongeth to them that are of full age, even those who by reason of use have their senses exercised to discern both good and evil." (Heb. 5:14) From the Concordant Literal N.T. (CLNT) we read from Hebrews 5:12-14, "For when also, because of time, you ought to be teachers, you have need again of one to teach you what are the rudimentary elements of the oracles of God, and you have to have need of milk, and not solid nourishment. For everyone who is partaking of milk is untrained in the word of righteousness, for he is a minor. Now solid nourishment is for the mature, who, because of habit, have faculties exercised for discriminating between the ideal and the evil."

Reading from Hebrews 6:1 "Therefore leaving the principles of the doctrine of Christ, let us go on unto perfection; not laying again the foundation of repentance from dead works, and of faith toward God, Of the doctrine of baptisms, and of laying on of hands, and of resurrection of the dead, and of eternal judgment."

These verses refer to, not the laying on of hands for healings or in ordination as Paul conferred on Timothy (1 Tim. 4:14). but to laying of hands on goats in ceremonial sacrifice. The perfect sacrifice of Jesus on the cross did away with animal sacrifices (Heb. 9:12-14).

The word "baptism" comes from the Greek word *baptismos, which means* immersion. It had to do with the ceremonial washing of pots and pans. That is also done away with in Christ. It is the same word as used in Matthew 7:4 and 8. Jesus condemned the Pharisees for their traditions of men. Mark 7:8, "For laying aside the commandment of God, ye hold the tradition of men, as the washing of pots and cups: and many other such like things ye do." The same word translated "washings" we find in Hebrews 9:10, "Which stood only in meats and drinks, and divers washings, and carnal ordinances, imposed on them until the time of reformation." In Jesus Christ we do away with ritual and embrace the reality.

We must first recognize a need to be taught, then be teachable and open to change, for this is essential to growth. Such teaching of the Word of God can come from studying different versions of the Bible, from tapes and literature of various ministries, from visiting various churches and from attending meetings where they preach a good solid Word. We may need to read some good Christian books, such as ones by Smith Wigglesworth. In the same sense that the Spirit of Jesus Christ continues to teach us, we must continue to learn. Above all, when we listen to the Holy Spirit as we study our Bible, He will direct us into all truth and reveal the meanings of the Scriptures to us. (John 16:13)

Spiritual maturity manifests in a child of God only through trials, processing, growth, and time. Our location on the road to spiritual maturity will help determine the quality of our walk. If we have matured spiritually, we will walk in the likeness of Jesus Christ and we will have grown up unto Him.

CHAPTER 7

▼

HOW TO WALK IN HIS STEPS

Jesus excels as our example in our Christian walk. He walked with purpose in everything He did or said. In the 21st Chapter of John, Jesus was cooking fish and bread (John 21:9) and invited His disciples to "come and dine." (v. 12) "Come" is an invitation and "to dine" was to eat of His flesh. Let us go one step further. "Come" is not a command nor is God forcing us to come and eat. It's an invitation. Now if we walk as He walked, then we too offer the invitation to others to come to us and dine. How do we do that? Not by telling people we are a Christian or telling them that we are a Kingdom or a manifested son.

Instead, our invitation is the life we live and the walk we walk, letting the Christ within us shine forth—in fact, if we shine forth so brightly, then we will easily attract people to us, and will be able to offer them spiritual food, which is ourselves. Many of us have been tried in the fire, just as the fish and the bread had been cooked by fire. Are we ready to feed them, to give them ourselves? Again, it is really the Christ within us.

Reading from 1 John 2:6 in the NAS version, "The one who says he abides in Him ought himself to walk in the same manner as He walked." The word "abide" (Greek: *memo*) means to abide, tarry, sojourn. From Word Studies in the Greek New Testament by Wuest (Vol. 2, p 1127): "...It's more than merely to position. It is used very often of a person abiding in a home, which implies fellowship, communion, dependence, and harmony. To abide in the Lord Jesus therefore implies not only position but relationship." "Ought" comes from the Greek word opheilo, and means to owe, to owe money, to be under obligation: bound by duty. "Walk" *(periteo)* means to conduct one's self, to order one's behavior. "To walk" is present infinitive in the Greek, emphasizing **habitual continuous action.** (Wuest)

Now Wuest's Expanded translation of 1 John. 2:6, "He who is constantly saying that he as a habit of life is living in close fellowship with and dependence upon Him, is morally obligated just as that One conducted Himself, also himself in the manner spoken of to be conducting himself."

How Beautiful the Feet.

We read in Romans 10:15, "And how shall they preach, except they be sent? as it is written, How beautiful are the feet of **them** that preach the gospel of peace, and bring glad tidings of good things!" Compare this to Isaiah 52:7 which states, "How beautiful upon the mountains are the feet of **him** that bringeth good tidings,..." Notice "them" and "him." Did Paul make a mistake? No! In Isaiah, "Him" refers to Jesus Christ, the Head, whereas the "them" in Romans refers to the many-membered body of Christ.

Does this refer to the beauty of literal feet? No! It means the way we **walk out** the life of Jesus Christ to the world. In other words, how beautiful is the walk of them that preach the gospel or preach a true gospel. This includes every believer in the life they lead, because they live the gospel. Or how beautiful is their life, the gospel or the good news that causes others to begin to desire in their own life. For example, if we see someone demonstrate godly gentleness, then we too desire to cultivate that same character that radiates from him or her.

In 1 Corinthians 12:23 we read, "...and our uncomely parts have more abundant comeliness." The word "comeliness " means elegance of figure, gracefulness. Our literal feet are uncomely but how beautiful or graceful are the feet or walk of them that preach the gospel of the Kingdom.

Peter reported in Acts 10:38, "How God anointed Jesus of Nazareth with the Holy Ghost and with power: who went about doing good, and healing all that were oppressed of the devil; for God was with him." Jesus was the Word personified. If we follow His walk, then we demonstrate what the Word of God says; we walk that life. It's the life we live, the walk we walk.

Our mortal flesh is the routine of our daily life, our daily walk, if you will. "For we who live are always delivered to death for Jesus' sake, that the life of Jesus also may be manifested in our mortal flesh." (2 Cor. 4:11 NKJV) That is the bottom line—that we manifest the life of Jesus in our daily life, including the way we act, think and talk.

Paul was praying for the Colossians, "That ye might **walk worthy** of the Lord unto all pleasing, being fruitful in every good work, and increasing in the knowledge of God." (Col. 1:10) "Walk" comes from the Greek word peripateo, to order one's behavior. "Worthy" translated from *axius*, means here: having the weight of another thing. It means something of life value or worth as much. The fruit bearing is a product of the knowledge of God.

Galatians 5:25 states, "If we live in the Spirit, let us also walk *(stoicheo)* in the Spirit." The word *stoicheo* means to walk in a straight line, to conduct one's self rightly. From Wuest, Vol. 12, p. 162: "The responsibility of the saint is to desire to live a Christian life, to depend upon the Holy Spirit for the power to live that life, and to step out in faith and live that life. This fulfilled will bring all the infinite resources of grace to the aid of the saint, and put in operation all the activities of the Spirit in his behalf." Notice that it is the Holy Spirit who gives us the power to walk the

Christian life, to walk in His steps. If we have been baptized in the Holy Spirit, then we have that power to use. (Acts 1:8)

The Lord Jesus Christ guides us in a walk that is like His. How do we know what to do? We listen to His voice. He speaks to us in many ways — through His word, through the still small voice in our spirit, through songs, through the written and spoken word, and through the actions of others. He said, "My sheep hear my voice, and I know them, and they follow me." (John. 10:27)

The Phillips translation of this verse reads, "My sheep **recognize** my voice and I know who they are." The Amplified says: "The sheep that are my own hear *and are listening to My voice*, and I know them and they follow Me." I believe a significant key to hearing His voice is to develop a **habit of listening to His voice.** Listening to His voice is not passive, but active. We must put forth spiritual effort to hear His voice.

Ah, as we tune out the clamor and the clang of the world around us, (literally and figuratively), as we *listen* to the "frequency" of Jesus Christ, we hear Him more and more when He speaks and thus He divinely guides us in our walk. It's like tuning into a certain radio frequency. The unsaved and some believers scoff at the idea of believers hearing God speak but pay no attention to them. You will be the one who will suffer for not obeying God. Just believe the Word of God.

To walk as Jesus walked doesn't mean that we follow His steps as a robot or "try" to follow Him with our natural mind and strength. It involves walking according to His nature under His divine guidance.

Remember that Abraham had several encounters in his life in which he made significant changes in his life. God told him, a heathen man, to leave his kindred and his country and go to an unknown land (Gen. 12:1). He obeyed the voice of God. Later God told him that he would make of thee a great nation (Gen. 12.2), When he laid his promised son on the altar and had even raised his knife to slay him, Abraham heard the voice of God to not harm his son for the sacrifice was in the thicket (Gen. 22:12). Each revelation that came to him came on his obedience to God's voice.

For us, we will not experience a fresh revelation of God in our life until we learn to obey that voice of God within us.

Scriptural Application

The Scriptures abound with examples and instructions on walking in the Kingdom. Let us examine one. "[Remember] this: he who sows sparingly *and* grudgingly will also reap sparingly *and* grudgingly, and he who sows generously *and* that blessing may come to someone, will also reap generously *and* with blessing." (2 Cor. 9:6 AMP) The previous text is speaking of giving money etc. but the principles apply to the whole spectrum of the Christian walk. He who gives of his money, time and talent sparingly to the Kingdom of God will reap sparingly and he who sows or gives generously will reap generously. If you do it grudgingly, however, that is with reluctance and with resentment (with your heart hanging on to that money), then you will reap grudgingly. The word "grudge" means to envy the possession or good fortune of another or to give or allow unwillingly and resentfully.

Let's apply this to all that we give to God. If we give so much time to God, whether small or large, if we give that time with reluctance, forever thinking of the "lost time" for ourselves and our plans, then that is giving it grudgingly. If, on the other hand, our local church asks for a special or heave offering and we give with a pure heart, without reluctance, then we will reap generously.

How many people can you count that you would give anything to them you had, with no strings attached or thought concerning of whether you'd get paid back? Those are the ones to whom you can give generously, without a grudge. It's a matter of giving our life, our money, our time and our all.

We expectantly give of ourselves to our spouse and our children or members of our immediate family, not sparingly or grudgingly. For example, what if our spouse says to us, "Honey, can you help me for a few minutes?" Unfortunately we are in the middle of a project of our own. What can we do? We have three choices. (1) We can say we're too busy. (2) We can help her (or him) grudgingly, or (3) We can help her (or him) with gladness. It's not really as important what we do as it is that we do it with the proper attitude. If we help our spouse with reluctance, then that is doing it grudgingly. If we help them with a pure and cheerful heart, sincerely wanting to please them, then that is giving generously, without compulsion, or is **walking** in Kingdom principles. The same principles hold for helping our brothers and sisters in Christ.

In Kingdom walking, first and foremost we consider love. We must always walk in love. Then we'll gain the doctrine if it's true. We don't try to force our doctrine on someone. On the other hand, we don't compromise or become wishy washy about our convictions and what the Scriptures really tell us. Neither do we lay aside our doctrine. It will find its place. We in the Body of Christ have made the word "doctrine" so negative, but it simply means "teaching." We will build the Kingdom in love. Love makes no distinction. "And **walk** in love, as Christ also hath loved us, and hath given himself for us an offering and a sacrifice to God for a sweet smelling savour." (Eph. 5:2)

Speaking of love, God's love for us is unconditional. It doesn't matter how much we have stumbled in our walk, how many times we have given up and said, "I can't walk the Christian walk, it's too difficult." No matter how many times we have walked away from God, He still loves us. Gods' love originates from Who He is. God is love. If we could grasp this and learn to walk in that truth, we'd be well ahead in our walk in the kingdom.

2 John 6 teaches, "And this is love, that **we walk after his commandments.** This is the commandment, That as ye have heard from the beginning ye should **walk** in it." From Wuest's Expanded Translation: "And this is the aforementioned love, namely, that we should be ordering our behavior dominated by His commandments. This is the commandment, just as you heard from the beginning, namely, that in its sphere you should be ordering your behavior."

"Walk in IT." The word "IT" refers to love, not commandments. The word "after" means according to. We are to walk and order our behavior, conducting ourselves dominated by the commandments of God. The Amplified reads, "...This is the commandment, as you have heard from the beginning, that you continue to walk in love—guided by it and following it."

1 John 5:3, Wuest: translation: "For this is the love of God, namely, that we are habitually and with solicitous care guarding and obsessing His commandment and His commandments are not burdensome."

Let us look to Jesus as an example of walking in the Kingdom and of His relationship to the Kingdom. Jesus is the Kingdom in person. You cannot separate the two. Jesus came into a world sick in spirit, soul and body. His miracles and healing power as He ushered in the Kingdom demonstrated the reality of the Kingdom of God. In the life of Jesus, especially during His three-and-one-half-year earthly ministry, the Kingdom became visible. He was not only dedicated to the Father, doing His will, but also dedicated to other human beings. He was the Son of God and the Son of Man.

Jesus was not against the Scriptures of the Old Testament but He found fault with the way the Jewish hierarchy interpreted them. They looked at the system through legalistic eyes and the letter of the law, while with Jesus it was mercy and compassion and the rights of man. Jesus came not to abolish the law but to fulfill it.

Jesus regarded the temple laws and dominion by the hierarchy as even more oppressive than the Roman government. In fact, He considered the temple government as it functioned as the exact opposite of the Kingdom He was bringing in. He told the Jews, "Destroy this temple and in three days I will raise it up. But he spake of the temple of his body." (John 2:19,21). In fact, the physical temple was destroyed in 70 A.D. The temple and all it stood for was central to the Jewish religion. But Jesus brought forth a better covenant and replaced Judaism with the Kingdom of God, which is an entirely different system (Heb. 8). Jesus became the final and perfect sacrifice for sin (Heb. 9).

Jesus did not shun the cross but sought it. Likewise, the mature, inner, spiritual man does not shun the workings of the cross but seeks them, for he knows that it is the cross that brings him to perfection. He knows that the cross will produce both fruit and holiness. In the works of the cross, God reveals to us our faults. When we operate at the foot of that cross, that is, always live in awareness of the meaning of the cross in our lives, we say, "Thank you Lord, for revealing that fault to me, I didn't realize it was displeasing to You." We know now that God revealed to us what to correct and how to correct it. We can also be confident that the Lord will help us to correct it. We will end up with a cleaner vessel and a purer walk. Furthermore, if we are mature Christians, we do not resent the chastisement, for we know that God produces pure, divine correction.

We know that the cross for Jesus brought resurrection in just three days. So for us, the resurrection is just three steps away. We lay our life down at the brazen altar in the outer court. We then walk just two more steps, one into the Holy Place and the next into the Holiest of Holies, the area of resurrection life. We can now walk in victory over that fault.

CHAPTER 8

▼

HOW UNIQUE IS OUR WALK

It's amazing how uniquely each person walks in the natural. Several years ago, for a period of four years, I taught at a unique, small, private, one year Junior College in New York. We had only 40 to 50 students, so I came to know all of them (all male) quite well. In the hallway outside my office we had tile or marble floors. I could distinctly hear each student's footsteps as they walked down the hall. Before we got very far into the school year, I could distinguish, with high accuracy, from my office, just by the sound of their footsteps, which student was walking along the hallway. Yes, our walk in the natural is very distinctive.

If our natural walk is unique, then how much more is our spiritual walk. We all have a unique background of both natural and spiritual experiences. At any given time, we are walking out something different or in different stages, whether blessings, corrections or trials or various facets of spiritual growth. But when we come together as living stones, we can draw on these unique strengths of each other—as we learn to tolerate and to embrace these differences as something to profit from rather than something to reject.

Walking in the Kingdom is first of all individual, then corporate. All the divine attributes and power that we require to rightly walk—in God—now dwell within us. Granted, some of these qualities, for now, reside in embryo form. Yet we now possess His divine nature. (2 Pet. 1:4) Each one of us, however, possesses unique ingredients. But the character, nature, grace and love of God has so many facets, it takes all of the body of Christ to manifest them. That is why we need to cultivate and manifest our individual spiritual strengths. God deals with each person differently or uniquely, even in apparent similar circumstances.

For example, God may be dealing with both you and your neighbor regarding your temper, but He will not deal with each of you in the same manner, for each of you walk a unique step and each of you dwells in a different place or position in God, each with differing experiences, and distinctive levels of commitment, and therefore your walks will be unique.

In the body of Christ, you are unique and your walk is unique. God needs you and the rest of the body needs you. (1 Cor. 12:20-22) The Baptist cannot say to the Pentecostal, "I have no need of thee;" neither can the Pentecostal say to the Baptist, "I don't need you". The mature in Christ can't say to the newborn babe, "I have no need of you." In the same way, those walking in the Holiest of Holies can't say to those in the Outer Court, "I don't need you."

We can't say to another, "I don't understand your walk. I can't see where you're walking. I can't keep step with you, therefore I can't (more likely, I won't) walk with you." We may not all walk alike or see eye to eye in doctrine but we can walk in harmony and in love and fellowship one another. (In fact, we are commanded to!) 1 John 5:2-3 tells us, "By this we know that we love the children of God, when we love God, and keep his commandments. For this is the love of God, that we keep his commandments: and his commandments are not grievous."

Relate to the body of Christ

The apostle Paul compares the body of Christ with our natural body (1 Cor. 12:12-27). Jesus is the head while the overcomers or feet company are the ones in contact with the earth. The feet company not only touch and walk on the earth (both the physical earth and the earth realm,) but they minister the Kingdom to others in the earth.

When the High Priest went through the Vail on the Day of Atonement, he was barefoot. That place was holy ground. The three parts of the High Priest visible as he passed through the veil were his head, his hands, and his feet. His robe hid his feet until he started walking. Likewise, we see Jesus Christ as the Head, and we see the five fold hand ministry in perfection. Then we see that same picture of glory in that feet company of overcomers, as it begins to walk out the truths of the kingdom, carries the entire Body of Christ through that same veil.

Now let us examine another aspect of the parts of the body of Christ. Paul relates, "If the foot shall say Because I am not the hand, I am not of the body..." The foot needs the hand ministry because it's the five fold ministry of the apostles, prophets, evangelists, pastors and teachers that bring this foot company into perfection here on earth.

In the next verse Paul mentions the eye and the ear. Those in the body who see revelations and visions must be subject to the "hearing" of the Word of the Lord. True faith comes only by this manner. They cannot say to the hand, I have no need of thee. The "eye" ministry may think they can sit at home and soak up great revelations and not need the hand ministry, but they are not in divine order. They must be willing to submit to the authority of the five-fold ministry. If not, they are headed for trouble. If a foreign object (false doctrine) gets into the eye, it takes the hand (five-fold ministry) to get it out, as rough and yet to be perfected as that hand may be.

If we isolate ourselves from the rest of the body of Christ because others don't believe just like we do, then we miss out on the chance for the joints and ligaments to fitly come together. (Eph. 4:16) Proverbs 18:1 NKJV reveals to us, "A man who isolates himself seeks his own desire; He rages against all wise judgment."

If you cut off our finger from your body, your finger will die. So if you cut yourself off from the body of Christ, you will die spiritually. However you do it, if you stop going to church, or stop fellowshipping with believers because they aren't perfect, the result is the same. Remember that true fellowship is based on the blood of Christ, not doctrine. The body of Christ needs your input and you need the input of the rest of the body.

As members in the Kingdom of God, each of us functions, with our varying talents, as unique individuals. We must view that individuality, not as a sign to go our own way, or to separate ourselves, but as an opportunity to serve, a responsibility to fit in with the rest of the body, and a determination to share our unique talents with the body of Christ. We must remember that though each of us is unique, our worth comes from God.

We need to share both our natural and spiritual talents with the rest of the body of Christ because all of us don't have skills for all things. If we have joy or peace, let's share it; if we have love, let's demonstrate it; when we have the gift to encourage others, let's prove it. Those who have the ability to fix cars might lend a hand and a wrench to help our brother or sister in need. Are you an artist? Then direct that talent to build up the rest of the body of Christ.

"For as we have many members in one body, and all members have not the same office." (Rom. 12:4) "Having then gifts differing according to the grace that is given to us, whether prophecy, let us prophesy according to the proportion of faith. Or ministry, let us wait on our ministering: or he that teacheth, on teaching; Or he that exhorteth, on exhortation: he that giveth, let him do it with simplicity; he that ruleth, with diligence; he that showeth mercy, with cheerfulness." (Rom. 12:6-8)

God not only created us but also has made us to express ourselves creatively. (Col. 1:16) These varied and unique creative desires seek to manifest themselves, not just in the arts, but in science, technology, personal relationships and our spiritual life. Part of our responsibility is to see that these creative expressions find fulfillment in positive ways that glorify God.

In America we strive to bring out the best in production or performance of our dogs, horses, cattle, poultry, sheep and other livestock, but why don't we do that for ourselves. In the past two decades we have come to deify average performance. What became of work ethic or going the second mile (Matt. 5:41) which means doing more than is required of us? God doesn't reward the slothful or the lazy. (Prov. 18:9; 2 Thess. 3:12; Heb. 6:12)

The strength of a nation and the Kingdom of God are never in the mediocrity of its members or its leadership but allowing all to pursue excellence, to reach for and grow toward God's best for them. I can think of nowhere in the Bible where God grants special rewards for average performance. We all have unique talents and abilities. Let's bring out the best of each one's potential. Let's strive to attain the best in those and encourage others to do the same, even our best in overcoming difficulties and in training our spirit to rule over our mind and body.

Just tolerating each other in the body of Christ isn't enough. Rather than concentrating on one another's faults, we ought to try to see the Christ within each other. Second, it's these unique differences, these unique qualities, that is, our different walk, thoughts, ideas, doctrines, or forms of worship that we need to accept. In balance, we don't automatically abandon our own doctrines without thought, study and prayer.

Now I believe this is a very important point for every believer to grasp. When we come together, whether it's one on one, in a small group, in our local assembly, in another church or at a convention, instead of rejecting our differences, we need to embrace those who believe somewhat differently among us in the body of Christ. We can then draw on their strengths and in turn give our strength to them. They may have something we need and vice versa. The eye can't say to the hand, I have no need of thee. We may even need to examine our own doctrine, or way of worship, or our own attitude to see if it fits in with the other parts of the body.

When we hear a preacher or teacher of the Word or listen to another believer one on one, let's not listen with a critical attitude, picking apart everything they say. Instead, let's listen with an open mind. If it's something we don't agree with, rather than flatly reject it, we can lay it on the shelf for further study—to see if it lines up with the Scriptures. The same principle applies to written Bible commentary or other Christian literature.

Paul wrote, "Let this mind be in you which was also in Christ Jesus." (Phil. 2:5) The mind that was in Christ Jesus was the Father's mind. Those who have the mind of Christ are the ones who have the mark of God, that is, the seal of the living God in their foreheads. Such a mark speaks not of a common brand, for it is invisible to man, but of one visible to the spirit of God.

Man by himself has tried for centuries to attain unity. He has tried teaching, dictatorships, social programs, compromises and even trying to avoid conflict. But he has never succeeded because natural minds are never one. Unity among the body of Christ and unity in the world come only when the carnal mind is crucified and the mind of God the Father comes to dwell in each of us as it dwelt in Jesus Christ. Then we experience true unity and true sonship.

We are first of all spirit beings, created by God. All of us sense and need not only to fellowship with God, spirit to Spirit, but with our fellow believers spirit to spirit. If we isolate ourselves from the rest of the body of Christ, we miss out on that intimacy so necessary for our complete well being. We could carry that one step further and say that a small local church that isolates itself from others in the body of Christ also misses out on what such fellowship would provide. I say "small church" because by chance alone, in a large local assembly, some members will interact with members of other churches. Remember that the first century church started with strong local churches or assemblies.

In balance, each one of us, on a daily basis, needs to sit down in a quiet time and meditate with God. Just let your mind become quiet. Let Him talk to you. Let the parade of ideas and thoughts march across your mind—what you did yesterday and what you need to be doing now. It takes practice. Yet in those quiet times, God will reveal Himself to you and may give you nuggets of divine wisdom for your daily life.

With each of us, starting at conception, God has formed a unique person. "For thou hast possessed my reins: thou hast covered me in my mother's womb." (Ps. 139:13) "My substance was not hid from thee, when I was made in secret, and curiously wrought in the lowest parts of the earth. Thine eyes did see my substance, yet being unperfect; and in thy book all my members were written, which in continuance were fashioned, when as yet there was none of them." (Ps. 139:15-16)

Some people spend their whole life struggling to change the way God made them. God knew what He was doing when He put you together. Be who you are. Be yourself. Who else is better qualified? Furthermore, when you operate in the realm of your capability, you will excel. Stop copying others, their place in the Kingdom or their ministry and enjoy being yourself. Concern yourself with being what God has called you to be, not what other people want you to be. That alone will make you unique, for each of us has a separate calling form God. No two people have the same fingerprints, the same DNA or the same voice print. What's more important, you can manifest the nature of God like nobody else can. Paul warned, "Don't let the world around you squeeze you into its own mold, but let God remold your minds from within..." (Rom. 12:2 Phillips)

From the moment of conception to old age, we must recognize the value and sanctity of life. The mentally and physically handicapped are precious in God's sight and are of infinite value to God. So we must recognize that same value. All have a unique role to play in the body of Christ.

Not all will rule and reign in the Kingdom, for each person is unique. "For as in Adam all die, even so in Christ shall all be made alive. But every man in his own order (turn)..."(1 Cor. 15:22-23) The Kingdom of God functions by degree. First you have Jesus and the court of 144,000 kings and priests (Rev. 7:4)—then the captains of the guards with the operation of the gifts. Next you have the priests—the 30 and 60 fold realms. Out on the fringes of the outer court it is dark. People there have been cast into outer darkness or a place void of spiritual understanding. (Matt. 22:13) This is not a geographical hell—what we have been taught in times past. But it is a living hell, however, a condition, right here on earth, right now, for people cut off from divine understanding. Such people walk in outer darkness. Yet many walk there because they chose to abandon the truth and walk away from God.

Walk in the Holiest

How do we walk in the Holiest of Holies, the area of deeper understanding and deeper truth? The same way we walk in the other realms—one step at a time, as we place the old ways under our feet.

The three compartments of the tabernacle reveal the three stages of glory that are available. So there are different degrees of glory in the body of Christ. A glory exists in the salvation realm (outer court) and for those who walk there. A greater glory is available for those who walk in the Pentecostal realm (The Holy Place), the realm of spiritual gifts and the light of the candlestick. For those who walk in the Holiest of Holies under the light (understanding) of the Shekinah glory of His presence, there is still a greater glory. Thus our walk is different or unique in each realm of our spiritual growth.

Do you remember the parable of the prodigal son? When he came to himself (realized he needed to turn around) (Luke 15:17), he would have been content to be one of his father's hired servants. (Luke 15:19) He said to his father, "I am not more worthy to be called thy son." (V. 21) V. 22 goes on to say, "But the father said to his servants, bring forth the best robe, and put it on him, and put a ring on his hands, and **shoes** on his feet." "Shoes" comes from the Greek word *hupodema* which means a shoe or sandal, something bound under the feet. "Sandal" (Acts 12:8) on the other hand, comes from the Greek word *sandalion* meaning slipper or sole pad. Royalty wore the shoes; the sandals by servants while the slaves generally went barefoot.

With the shoes come responsibility—to walk worthy of the Kingdom. The shoes symbolize authority (to rule), to walk as royalty in the Kingdom. It's not something we do just on Sunday morning. First of all, as a son, we rule over our own house (mind, emotions and body) by our spirit and we keep our flesh under control. On the other hand, a servant walks in the protection of the king's household but doesn't share in the inheritance, privileges and authority of the Kingdom. Thus, his walk differs from the son or heir.

When we start a new project or new employment quite different from previous ones we've experienced, it may take time to walk it out—to learn the new ways, skills, policies and requirements of the new job. In a similar way, when we go through financial problems, the Lord may have us walk out each situation different than the previous ones. Or suddenly we're unemployed—how do we walk that out—the finances, the budgeting, and the heartache? On the other hand, suppose we get a much higher paying job? Do we increase our standard of living? Do we waste money on luxuries or can we walk it out as a good steward? We talk not about a futuristic Disney World kingdom out in the sky but a Kingdom of God here and now on earth.

Walk by Faith

"For we walk by faith [that is, we regulate our lives and conduct ourselves by our conviction or belief respecting man's relationship to God and divine things, with trust and holy fervor, thus we walk] not by sight *or* appearance." (2 Cor. 5:7 AMP)

Many Christians would like to get to the place where they wouldn't have to **walk** by faith or live by faith. They would like someone to give them a million dollars so that they wouldn't have to believe God for finances. They would like to be living in divine health or divine life so that they wouldn't have to believe or have the faith for healing. Others would like the best of material possessions or material blessings in cars, homes, appliances, and computers—so that they don't have to believe God or walk by faith in that area of their life. That is the wrong reason for living in divine life. Seek ye first the Kingdom of God and His righteousness.

Someone who has never been sick in his or her life may, later in life, have a hard time believing God for healing. Yet we must be careful how we talk to one who struggles with such a problem. We may have never had that particular problem or we may have conquered it with ease. We could say to them, "It's simple, just believe, and just start walking it out." For them, it may not be that simple. For example, in my own life, by the grace of God, I have never taken on the habit of smoking, so except by divine wisdom, I can't relate to someone struggling to give up cigarettes.

Inquire of the Lord

The book of 2nd Samuel describes David's encounter with the Philistines. He didn't assume that he was to fight the enemy in the same way as he did the last time or even fight them at all. He first asked the Lord for assurance that the Lord was going into battle with him, and second, he asked for directions in the battle. Rather than inquire of the Lord in our walk, we so often move ahead of Him. Many believers try to solve their problems their own way, rather than seeking God for His will in the matter.

Let us inquire of the Lord each day, asking Him, "Lord, what can you use me for today? How can I be of service to you today?" We don't wait for a crisis (battle) or problems in our life, but ask each day. Prior to each church service we attend, we might ask the Lord, "Lord, how could I be of service to you today in this meeting, that You might be glorified?"

We may be aware of many spiritual problems, but the Lord has a time and method to conquer each one. He wants us to seek Him that He might direct and guide us through the battle. For example, you have a habit of interrupting people when they are talking. The one who doesn't have that problem or has overcome it may say, "That's simple, just quit interrupting. It's not that simple for many people. The Lord may have a different method for each time that you need to walk out the victory over this habit, just as He may have a different method for you to walk out the other areas in your life. You need to seek Him, even for proper attitude toward each problem and how to walk out each problem. You must also ask God for His strength.

When we win the battle over the enemy (or circumstances) as David did, we have just begun. We must **walk out** that victory and that territory. Joshua won battles over his enemies but he, his armies, and the Israelites had to **walk out the land** to possess it. God told Joshua, "Every place that the sole of your foot shall tread upon, that have I given unto you, as I said unto Moses." (Josh. 1:3).

CHAPTER 9

▼

How to Walk in the Tabernacle

How does an individual believer advance from the outer court (30-fold realm) to the Most Holy Place (100-fold realm)? Each realm of or walk requires a different step, a different gait or stride, even a different lifestyle. In the Outer Court, there are 30 steps (1-30) after the initial salvation experience. When we advanced from the Outer Court to the Holy Place (60-fold realm or 31 to 60) we learned new steps, a new way to walk. We sought the Lord to guide us in this new walk. We moved from the salvation experience to the Pentecostal experience.

Now in the Holy Place we no longer walk by natural light (understanding) but by the light of the candlestick (Holy Spirit). Here we had looked at Jesus as Saviour but now see Him as the Christ, The Anointed. Our travels took us out of Egypt into a wilderness experience. We walked as workers but now walk as warriors. Now we no longer walk as children who drink milk do but now we walk as the more mature, eating bread.

From walking in divine healing, we advance to walking in divine health. In the outer court God saved our spirit, now He saves our soul. Before we bore some fruit, but now, we bear more fruit. From little faith in the 30-fold realm believers grow to great faith in the 60- fold realm. A very important point, we advanced from new birth to the Holy Spirit baptism.

To advance in the realm of the Holy Place, we take 30 major steps. Each step has a purpose; each step involves a new experience of Jesus Christ manifesting Himself in us and through us. Sorry, no short cuts. Just as we can't reach the Most Holy Place from the Outer Court without passing through the Holy Place (and that experience), nor can we skip from step 32 to 35. At step 32 we might catch a glimpse of a resting-place at 35 but we can't get there without taking steps 33 and 34. It's part of a process.

In the Most Holy Place, we now look forward to the salvation of our body (to be redeemed). Stepping into the Most Holy Place (100-fold realm), the brightness of the light of the candlestick (of the Holy Place) fades as we begin to walk in the divine light (divine understanding) of the Shekinah (Rev. 22:5). We walk now in the Feast of Tabernacle Experience! In this realm we look to Jesus now as Lord more than the Christ. In each area of our life in which we allow The Lord Jesus Christ to rule, He is Lord over that part of our life. Furthermore, "...no man can say that Jesus is the Lord, but by the Holy Ghost." (1 Cor. 12:3) We walk out of the wilderness into the land (symbolizing the Promised Land). (Amos 2:10) Now we walk as a worshipper rather than a warrior. (John 4:23) and walk more like a mature son (Heb. 5:14). We now bear much fruit and grow from great faith to all faith. From Holy Spirit baptism we advance to maturity.

In this realm we replace our diet of bread with strong meat or solid spiritual nourishment. (Heb. 5:14) We walk more in divine life rather than divine health. We no longer give tithes; we are a tithe. To be a tithe means we give our entire life over to God. Our walk emerges from the acceptable to the perfect will of God. Again, we seek the Lord for each step of the way, for it is a new walk. And again, advancing in the 100-fold realm is a process beginning with step 61 through step 99 to 100. We won't be perfected (become fully mature) until we have walked each step.

We read in Psalms 103:7, "He made known his ways unto Moses, his acts unto the children of Israel." As we walk from the outer court, through the Holy Place, then on to the Most Holy Place, we press forward from knowing His acts (external) (outer court or salvation), to knowing His ways (internal) (Holy Place or Pentecostal experience) to *being* (His nature) (Most Holy Place or Feast of Tabernacles experience). *Being* is of a higher order or more advanced walk than either *doing* or watching. Mary sat at the feet of Jesus while Martha busied herself and fussed over food preparation (Luke 10:39). Our lesson is this. Sitting at the feet of Jesus, absorbing His Word and taking on His nature is more important or of a higher order than doing (something) or seeing only of what God has done (His acts).

In the Kingdom of God, we advance one step at a time. Just as we passed first grade before we could enter the second grade, or we finished elementary school before we entered high school, so it is in the Kingdom. If we don't take those first steps, we cannot take the latter steps. Every lesson we skip or neglect, we will have to go back and learn it before we can move on. Many Christians have never advanced into the higher realms of God because they haven't taken the foundational steps or those steps that God called them to go through. Many want to skip from their salvation experience to the Most Holy Place without going through the Pentecostal experience. That is impossible. It does not follow the pattern of the Scriptures. In each step, to advance in the Kingdom, we go through learning, understanding, pruning, purging, cleansing, overcoming, commitment, testing, obedience and processing.

God looks at the whole man, his heart, as to his faithfulness, commitment and obedience. In some areas of our spiritual life we may dwell at the 90-fold level, maybe in others only the 35 fold level. But our overall being may be at the 65-fold level.

On the other hand, I do not despise my salvation or Pentecostal experiences, just as I don't despise my experiences or the things I learned in elementary or high school. But I move on to higher things in God.

Our Comfort Zone

Two major lessons can be learned from the above discussion of the tabernacle. One, we must not assume that each time we go into battle against the enemy that the Lord will tell us to fight it the same way nor would He have us walk it out the same way. Each realm and each step within that realm is different.

Second, we can't get so comfortable in our place or walk in God, so self confident on how we walked from step 62 to 63 and to 64, that we don't need God for step 65. We can't get so comfortable or so "self" confident in the things we do on our job, or using the machines, typewriters, or computers we operate, that we don't need to seek and rely on God for those tasks. We can't feel so comfortable in raising our children that we don't need the Lord for the next decision in guiding them. Sometimes God will "direct us" in such a way to show us that He wants us to get out of our comfort zone, especially when He wants us to do something different.

We even may have become comfortable in the old personality traits of our past, such as impatience, anger, strife, critical spirit or arrogance, which are marks of someone who hasn't walked far into the tabernacle (toward the Holiest of Holies),—that is, one who fails to demonstrate the attributes of the 100-fold realm.

Sometimes God has already purposed the space for that next step. He's just waiting for us to take that step. Walking in the Kingdom of God may pull us out of our present comfort zone. It is easier sometimes to just sit back and let others do the witnessing, easier to just hang on to our past doctrines than to study the scriptures to see if these new ones are true. It's sometimes easier to let the flesh rule and eat that extra piece of cake, or to speak that harsh word rather than to hold our tongue. It takes effort to forgive or effort to swallow our pride and say, "I'm sorry, I was wrong." Isaiah 60:1, exhorts us to "Arise, shine; for thy light is come, and the glory of the LORD is risen upon thee." We need to arise from where we are and step up to the next point in God. He wants to prove to us who He is and who we are. We may even find that once we have ventured out from our present comfort zone to reach to higher heights in God, that turning back is no longer an option. We may have tasted some of the deeper truths of God, some of which may run contrary to what we had been taught. It is risky. But we can't turn back.

Studying one aspect of our comfort zone, we might consider King Solomon. Solomon's downfall was that under the influence of his many wives, fell into the trap which led to the introduction of false gods into Jerusalem. (1 Kings 11:1-8)

The Laodecian church was passive. (Rev. 3:15) Those of that persuasion are comfortable in their present position in God. They say, " this far" but no further. It is part of our nature to prefer the familiarity and security of the known. Why is this? It's because many of us regard the unknown as a threat rather than a hope.

In our comfort zone we find it easier to ignore the unlovable, rather than to show love to someone we may not even "like" in the natural. We may find it easier to retaliate when hurt, because that's our carnal nature, if not under control of the spirit. It's easier to let fear, doubt, or unbelief run its course, than to rise up in faith when trouble comes. We may have been so used to these thought patterns, that we have become comfortable in such a frame of mind.

We probably feel comfortable with certain habits, ideas, philosophies of life, ways of doing things, ways of thinking, even bad spirits, the way we walk and where we walk, even in our place in God. We may think it's too much mental effort to grasp on to new spiritual truths, afraid to let go of our past false teaching and the traditions of men. When we advance from one realm to the next, we may get so comfortable in one realm or place in our life, that we get spiritually lazy and refuse to take the next step.

Some of the Israelites in the wilderness drove down their tent stakes and refused to move with the cloud. As result, they died in the wilderness, because the manna and the blessings of God ceased at that place. In their comfort zone, some bowed to other gods. (Num. 25:1) Rebellion against God sometimes resulted in death. (Num. 16:32) Except for Joshua and Caleb and the next generation, they all died in the wilderness. (Num. 14:31-32) "Now all these things happened unto them for ensamples: and they are written for our admonition, upon whom the ends of the world are come." (1 Cor. 10:11).

Just as we encounter different ways to walk in the 100-fold realm as contrasted to the 60 fold, each major step is a new experience. In balance, we need **not** seek the Lord for every minute detail in our lives. For example, some believers think that they need to seek the Lord every day for what dress or suit to wear, or whether to buy cabbage or lettuce at the grocery store. That isn't what we are talking about. If we walk by the leading of the Spirit of God (Rom. 8:14), then if by chance that dress or suit does make a difference, we will know it by our spirit.

A basic principle from the field of physical education states that in order to increase strength, we must do more than is comfortable or easy. When we push beyond our comfort zone by lifting weights or by doing more repetitions, or jogging faster, our muscular, skeletal and aerobic capabilities develop. We can apply this same principle to our spiritual development. The more we push beyond our present limits, the more we grow spiritually. We may impose limitations *on ourselves* but God doesn't withhold any good thing. If we would just stretch our spiritual muscles, He has more for us than we can imagine.

In 1996 I sprained my shoulder and upper arm at work. Since I couldn't raise my left arm very high or very far to the side, I went to a physical therapist. He instructed me to exercise several times a day to strengthen and stretch those tightened muscles. He finally told me that when I exercised that arm, I needed to stretch my arm beyond the comfort zone, that is, **beyond** the point where it began to hurt. Likewise, if we would choose to push beyond what we think our spiritual limit is, we would most likely grow much more rapidly in the Kingdom of God.

Personal Applications of Walking

In our walk, if we wait for perfect conditions or perfect knowledge, we will never take that next step. The Psalmist said, "Thy word is a lamp unto my feet...." (Ps. 119:105). That is just enough light (understanding) for one step. In the natural, when we walk in the dark with a flashlight, we shine it just ahead of us, to the place of our next step. So many times in our spiritual walk, we want to see far ahead to see whether or not we want to walk that way. In other words, we seek God's will way out in front of us, far into our future. But God doesn't reveal His will to us for us *to consider.*

We strive to walk out the attributes of God that He has placed within us. We have the incorruptible seed of Christ within us. Let's break down that middle wall of partition, that wall that is made of old doctrines, sayings, habits, thought patterns, and beliefs. Walking in the Kingdom isn't about walking in a doctrine but about walking in Jesus Christ. We continue to build our own life with the guidance and help of the Lord and the Word of God. "If we live in the Spirit, let us also walk in the Spirit." (Gal. 5:25)

God outlines the qualifications necessary for priesthood, for those who offered the bread (Word) of God in the book of Leviticus, the 21st chapter. Leviticus deals with the physical handicaps that would disqualify a priest. Today, we deal with spiritual priesthood. It's not the natural handicaps, but the spiritual handicaps that may disqualify us from preaching the word of God. We don't confine preaching to the pulpit but refer to living and walking righteously in the Kingdom, living the life of Christ.

A priest who has good eyesight but is lame is described in verse 18 of the 21st chapter. Such a person today can discern what God is doing and God's purpose for the body of Christ. What's more, he sees wonderful revelation truths. He can talk a great message or speak great things from the Scriptures. But unfortunately he is lame, so he can't walk out what he sees or speaks. Because he has trouble following Jesus, he sets a poor example before other people. He can tell you how to live in victory but he usually falls short of it in his own life.

Consider the man who was lame from birth that Peter and John met in Acts chapter 3. Many Christians today, from the time they were "born again," have never really walked a good Christian walk, (never very consecrated) and have committed little to God. Sadly they have never really even started to walk the Christian walk after salvation.

Peter and John saw that the man needed something besides alms or treasures. They ministered to his need to walk, a much greater need. Many today, like the lame man trying to fill his cup with alms, hop from one church to the next, hoping to fill their mind (their tin cup) with spiritual knowledge. But they haven't yet learned how to walk in the Kingdom. If they would accept the deeper spiritual truths and put Kingdom walking into practice, they would no longer seek nor need the alms.

Wait Upon the Lord

Consider Isaiah 40:31, "But they that wait upon the LORD shall renew their strength; they shall mount up with wings as eagles; they shall run, and not be weary; and they shall walk, and not faint." To "wait" on the Lord does not mean to sit around and do nothing, waiting for Him to speak to us or to give us new direction. I hear many discuss this verse as if it means that if we wait, then God will show us His will in that matter. God's will for our lives is His Word.

The word "wait" here means to be intertwined. To wait on the Lord then means to be intertwined with Him, His nature and His plan and purpose for our lives. The word "eagles" speaks of eagle saints or overcomers. To "mount up" means that we are caught up to the throne room power.

Let us examine two other related verses. "Commit thy way unto the LORD; trust also in him; and he shall bring it to pass." (Ps. 37:5) "For evildoers shall be cut off: but those that wait upon the LORD, they shall inherit the earth." (Ps. 37:9)

From these three verses (including Isaiah 40:31), the Bible teaches dependence rather than delay. That is, we trust and expect the Lord and His Kingdom will triumph over the situation, that we might inherit that portion of the earth. This is victory over things of the earth realm here and now, not in the sweet by and by.

In our natural life, we drive our car along a road and see signs, that say, "curve, 45 mph" or "bridge out" or "pavement ends" or "wrong way" or we come to a signal light. We gladly accept these warnings and appreciate them as absolutely necessary for our safety. Yet, when it comes to spiritual matters, we often resent warnings from God.

Many often resent God warning them by His Word or through another believer that they are on the wrong course, going too fast or need to change spiritual direction. But if we would hunger and thirst for righteousness, then we will be fulfilled, totally satisfied, for God wants us to be fulfilled. He often guides us by corrections. Sometimes it's by chastisement. If He didn't chastise us, we'd be as bastards. (Heb. 12:8) Warnings we receive from Him are not legalistic, but is God displaying His love. He is warning us of our wrong attitude or our wrong ways for our own good. He isn't trying to spoil our fun—He is simply trying to keep us from getting hurt, spiritually, emotionally, financially or physically.

Back Off

Proverbs 4:24-27, NKJV. "Put away from you a deceitful mouth, And put perverse lips far from you. (25). Let your eyes look straight ahead, And your eyelids look right before you. (26) Ponder the path of your feet, And let all your ways (of thinking and living) be established. (27) Do not turn to the right or the left; Remove your foot (your walk) from evil." (Parentheses this author).

Verse 26 in the NIV version states: "Make level paths for your feet and take only ways that are firm." The Moffatt Bible translates v. 27, "Never turn to right or left, draw back from a wrong step."

What do these verses mean? Our mouth, lips, eyes and feet are physical symbols for speaking, for what we see or observe, and for our walk or conduct. These verses mean to back off, draw back, or nip in the bud any time negative or ungodly thoughts, even thoughts of condemnation, enter our mind. When we allow negative thoughts about circumstances or people to linger in our mind, we just open the door for more negative thoughts. An accumulation of these thoughts leads to resentment, fault finding, depression, pity parties, and eventually bitterness. To eliminate some of this negative influence, we cultivate friends who agree with us on positive things.

Our actions or what we do with our feet, in turn first arise from our thoughts. An evil, negative or contrary thought from our own mind or from another person must not sidetrack us—we must stick to those principles grounded in the Word of God.

Returning to verse 25 of the 4th chapter of Proverbs—we must not be distracted by those thoughts that would try to "come in from the side,"—ones that would detract us from our mission. We can't entertain the thoughts that are contrary to our spiritual goals. Verse 26 tells us to consider and think about the way and direction you walk. Godly principles and the Word should establish this. The word "ways" refers to activities, and projects—our general philosophy of life, how we live and conduct ourselves. We must be firm in our conviction—not wishy-washy. If we base our convictions on the Word of God, we won't deviate. Verse 26 of the Amplified Bible says it this way: "Consider well the path of your feet, and let all your ways be established *and* ordered aright."

The NAS expresses verse 27, "Do not turn to the right nor to the left; Turn your foot from evil." This means to quickly back off any time our actions, words or thoughts run contrary to the Word of God. It is easy to get trapped into speaking negative words, especially when we fellowship those who habitually speak negative statements about circumstances, or other people. "Right or left" means: do not take your focus off the right-eous path. A little compromise here and there takes you to the left or the right. "Ponder and consider" (v. 26) means: take a conscious note of the path you are walking. Stop often to consider- is this a godly action/direction to be going? Will what I say or do hurt someone or will it lift them up? Will it strengthen the body of Christ? "Path"—includes what you are doing or saying to children or spouse, brother or sister in Christ. Does it edify them or could it be left unsaid?

Walking in the three parts of the tabernacle, or through the three experiences of the believer, is a step by step process, from step one to step 100. We have advanced from the outer court (30 fold) to the Holy Place (60 fold), to the Most Holy Place (100 Fold). But from this highest realm, it's no time or place for arrogance or neglect to help those in the 30 and 60 fold realms. We can't develop into "bless me" clubs. If someone comes to us needing salvation, we minister to him or her. If they need the baptism of the Holy Spirit, we minister to them. Whatever their natural or spiritual need, as the Lord leads, we must help them. Our pattern springs from the Old Testament High Priest, who came back out from the Most Holy Place to minister to the people.

CHAPTER 10

▼

RANK IN THE KINGDOM

Is God a respecter of persons? "Why, of course not, " you say. Under all conditions? Let's examine the Scriptures. Some people quote part of the scripture, "'God is no respecter of persons,' therefore...." Then they add whatever they desire to that portion, whether it is some belief of Scripture or some current situation in their life. Some people say that since God is no respecter of persons, all people are (or "will be," if they are futuristic in their belief) equal in the Kingdom. Therefore, they say, "If God blessed Charlie with a new car, I should get one too." Or "God blessed Susie with healing; therefore He should heal me too." Or "God advanced Joe in the ministry; therefore He should advance me." These things aren't necessarily so.

Let's examine the Scriptures, especially the context, to see what they really mean. From Acts 10:34, "Then Peter opened his mouth, and said, Of a truth I perceive that God is no respecter of persons:"

Definition: "respecter"- denotes a biased judgment, which gives respect to rank, position, or circumstances instead of considering the intrinsic condition. It means that God shows no respect (partiality) in justice, judgment, or favorable treatment when dealing with people.

Let's examine a few more scriptures. Proverbs 28:21 says, "To have respect of persons is not good:..." Romans 2:9-13 tells us: "Tribulation and anguish, upon every soul of man that doeth evil, of the Jew first, and also of the Gentile; But glory, honour, and peace, to every man that worketh good, to the Jew first, and also to the Gentile: For there is no respect of persons with God. For as many as have sinned without law shall also perish without law: and as many as have sinned in the law shall be judged by the law; For not the hearers of the law are just before God, but the doers of the law shall be justified."

The above verse confirms a message of salvation to both the Jew and the Gentile (Greek). Whosoever shall call on the name of the Lord shall be saved, both Jew and Greek. As to salvation, God shows no respect of persons. But the above verses say nothing about rank in the Kingdom or how God deals with those after they are saved.

From the Old Testament, we read, "Ye shall do no unrighteousness in judgment: thou shalt not respect the person of the poor, nor honour the person of the mighty: but in righteousness shalt thou judge thy neighbour" (Lev. 19:15) Again, here, respect of persons has to do with righteous judgment, not rank in the kingdom. "It is not good to have respect of persons in judgment." (Prov. 24:23)

What about the Jew or Greek? We read in Romans 10:12-13, "For there is no difference between the Jew and the Greek: for the same Lord over all is rich unto all that call upon him. For whosoever shall call upon the name of the Lord shall be saved." Here God shows that He grants no favoritism to either a Jew or Gentile as to glory, honor, peace, or to one that worketh good.

"Servants, be obedient to them that are your masters according to the flesh, with fear and trembling, in singleness of your heart, as unto Christ." (Eph. 6:5) "And, ye masters, do the same things unto them, forbearing threatening: knowing that your Master also is in heaven; neither is there respect of persons with him." (Eph. 6:9)

In these two verses, Paul writes about servants and masters. He instructs us to show no respect of persons because of their rank, whether master or servant. A master is just as responsible to live righteously as a servant is. In today's world, an employer or employee, people in top management or those with the blue collar, corporation president or janitor, are all responsible to live righteously. The same principle holds true for husband and wife, parents and children. None can be slothful in their Christian walk, either at work or at home.

James wrote, "My brethren, have not the faith of our Lord Jesus Christ, the Lord of glory, with respect of persons. For if there come unto your assembly a man with a gold ring, in goodly apparel, and there come in also a poor man in vile raiment; And ye have respect to him that weareth the gay clothing, and say unto him, Sit thou here in a good place; and say to the poor, Stand thou there, or sit here under my footstool: Are ye not then partial in yourselves, and are become judges of evil thoughts?" (Jas. 2:1-4)

Here James tells us not to show respect or partiality because one is rich or poor. Again, a rich man as well as a poor man is required to live righteously, to receive no special favors because of wealth. If we promote a person to an office or position in our local church just because they are rich, then we show respect of persons.

God chooses whom He will

The book of Genesis discusses the differences between two unequal brothers, Cain and Abel. What about Abraham and his nephew Lot? They had pooled their herds and flocks that grazed together. But the herds finally became so large, that they had to divide them. Abraham gave Lot his choice of the hills or the plains. Lot (representing the flesh) chose the plains, the easy way out, that which appeals to the eyes and to the flesh. This account illustrates an important Kingdom principle. In the

Kingdom, what appeals to the flesh is usually not the way God wants us to go. Lot eventually ended up in Sodom and Gomorah.

Abraham, on the other hand, took the hills and rocks where he would face more hardships and would have to dig wells. But he trusted God who did provide for him. God had instructed him to leave his kindred, and then when he finally parted from Lot, God told him to look unto the hills. When we leave our fleshly desires (Lot) behind, then God reveals Himself to us. He will reveal spiritual truth and spiritual guidelines in our day to day life in the Kingdom. Therefore, from the account of Abraham, we conclude that God chose him out of a multitude of people and blessed him with more than He blessed Lot.

At another time God, through the prophet Samuel, chose David, the youngest of seven brothers to anoint, raise and train to become the King of Israel. God chose Joseph, the second to the youngest son of Jacob to save his family and relatives from the famine and as second in command to Pharaoh, to direct the country of Egypt in their time of plenty and of famine.

Other accounts in the Scriptures demonstrate how God showed respect of persons or favoritism. Certain saints God called above their contemporaries to leadership roles, including Elisha (1 Kings 9:19) after Elijah had cast his mantle upon him. In the New Testament, God also appeared to the apostle Paul "....to make thee a minister and a witness..." (Acts. 26:16) "....a preacher, apostle, teacher (2 Tim. 1:11). We read in John 15:16 where God has chosen us. "Ye have not chosen me, but I have chosen you, and ordained you, that ye should go and bring forth fruit, and that your fruit should remain: that whatsoever ye shall ask of the Father in my name, he may give it you." We are made able ministers of the New Testament. (2 Cor. 3:6)

Jesus chose 12 disciples from a cross-section of the prevailing political, social and religious systems, and from a wide range of personalities and temperaments. According to Mark 1:17, "And Jesus said unto them, Come ye after me, and I will make you to become fishers of men." In reference to James and John, "And straightway he called them: and they left their father Zebedee in the ship with the hired servants, and went after him." (Mark 1:20)

Jesus also showed respect when He fed the 5,000 by ordering them to sit down in ranks. Mark 6:39-40, "And he commanded them to make all sit down by companies upon the green grass. And they sat down in ranks, by hundreds, and by fifties." (See also Luke 9:14).

God can choose any person of any "status" to train and promote to a position of "leadership" or to any other office that He desires. "But when thou art bidden, go and sit down in the lowest room; that when he that bade thee cometh, he may say unto thee, Friend, go up higher: then shalt thou have worship in the presence of them that sit at meat with thee." (Luke 14:10) It's God who may choose us to advance to a higher position.

In the Kingdom, God considers people of infinite value so will place them in a calling that He desires. Those working behind the scenes—the intercessors,—and such as those with the gift of helps, God considers just as important as the preachers, evangelists and apostles, song leaders or those in front as "leaders." We can say the same for "leaders" in the business world. "And the eye cannot say unto the hand, I have no need of thee: nor again the head to the feet, I have no need of you." (1 Cor. 12:21)

When much is given, much is required. To those who receive more, such as ministers placed in authority, God gives more responsibility. "But he that knew not, and did commit things worthy of stripes, shall be beaten with few stripes. For unto whomsoever much is given, of him shall be much required: and to whom men have committed much, of him they will ask the more." (Luke 12:48) In the first century church, the disciples had the most responsibility to preach the gospel. "My brethren, be not many masters, knowing that we shall receive the greater condemnation." (Jas. 3:1) And in Hebrews 3:17, "But with whom was he grieved forty years? was it not with them that had sinned, whose carcasses fell in the wilderness?" Here God showed a respect of persons.

When we read Romans 8:14, "As many as are led by the Spirit..." it indicates that not all are led by the Spirit, and indicates a group set apart.

Also notice a comment Peter made in the following Scripture, "Him (Jesus) God raised up the third day, and showed him openly; Not to all the people, but unto witnesses chosen before of God, even to us, who did eat and drink with him after he rose from the dead." (Acts 10:40-41). Notice the phrase, "not to all the people."

God, even today, reveals secrets to those who function in the office of a prophet that He doesn't reveal to others in the body of Christ. The prophets aren't necessarily those who just prophesy but also others called by the Lord God for their leadership role in the Kingdom. "Surely the Lord GOD will do nothing, but he revealeth his secret unto his servants the prophets." (Amos 3:7) Thus, God shows respect of persons concerning the revealing of secrets.

The Leadership of Moses

Let us look briefly at part of the life of Moses. Jethro, the father-in-law of Moses, spoke to Moses concerning rank and order. Exodus 18:21-23 reads, "Moreover thou shalt provide out of all the people able men, such as fear God, men of truth, hating covetousness; and place such over them, to be rulers of thousands, and rulers of hundreds, rulers of fifties, and rulers of tens: And let them judge the people at all seasons: and it shall be, that every great matter they shall bring unto thee, but every small matter they shall judge: so shall it be easier for thyself, and they shall bear the burden with thee. If thou shalt do this thing, and God command thee so, then thou shalt be able to endure, and all this people shall also go to their place in peace."

The account of Moses here speaks of order, rank, delegated authority, and submission in the Kingdom of God. Fifty is the basic unit in which members can relate to one another. Those in charge of the 1000 judge the weightier matters. Moses' task was still weightier. In the Kingdom today, God calls some to look after the small matter of a few, but they don't mind that role. They often have the gift to discern the detail and the personal matters that need attention. The people God calls for these small matters become skillful at them and become valuable and necessary in the Kingdom. They need not feel inferior.

God calls others to judge the weightier matters of the Kingdom. This latter group often sees the more extensive viewpoint or scope of a matter. In a local church, these people see the vision or direction not only for the local assembly but also for the region or for the body of Christ as a whole. This account teaches humility. Moses was meek or teachable, even in the sight of God, no matter how high in rank.

God chooses many in the Kingdom as instruments for His purpose. Yet there is a definite order of (1) servants, (2) friends, and (3) the chosen. For example, in Haggai 2:23, "In that day, saith the LORD of hosts, will I take thee, O Zerubbabel, my servant, the son of Shealtiel, saith the LORD, and will make thee as a signet: for I have **chosen** thee, saith the LORD of hosts."

In the New Testament we read from John 15:15, "Henceforth I call you not servants; for the servant knoweth not what his lord doeth: but I have called you **friends**; for all things that I have heard of my Father I have made known unto you." In John 15:16 we read, "Ye have not chosen me, but I have **chosen** you, and ordained you, that ye should go and bring forth fruit, and that your fruit should remain: that whatsoever ye shall ask of the Father in my name, he may give it you."

Jesus chose 12 Disciples

What do other Scriptures say concerning rank in the Kingdom of God? . Do we find examples of ranks or do the scriptures declare that all are equal under all conditions in the Kingdom? Again, let us examine the scriptures. Jesus is often described in the gospels as speaking to the "multitude." These multitudes were ones that at least followed Him. They heard His teaching, received His healing power and saw His miracles. To them He spoke in parables. Those who stayed behind heard or saw nothing first hand. Luke 10:1 tells us that Jesus **appointed** seventy from out of the multitude to go and minister. Luke 10:1 KJV, "After these things the Lord appointed other seventy also, and sent them two and two before his face into every city and place, whither he himself would come." We also note that God instructed Moses to choose seventy elders to go to the top of the mountain to worship. (Exod. 24:1)

Jesus **chose** the 12 disciples to whom He explained the parables and taught the deeper truths. They didn't volunteer; rather Jesus chose them. They walked close with Him for three and one-half years. Next He had the inner circle of three—Peter, James, and John. These three are mentioned together in ten New Testament verses. Can we not say then that Jesus showed respect of persons in choosing first the 12 and then the three?

Some people don't want to hear the deeper truths, simply because they realize that it will require of them to lead a more disciplined life, so they just refuse to listen. Proverbs 15:32 states, "He that refuseth instruction despiseth his own soul: but he that heareth reproof getteth understanding." Thus we have a distinction or respect of persons between those who heed instruction and those who don't. In natural matters, I have known many people who refused to try simple natural remedies to improve their health. They simply refused instruction.

Jesus chose to teach just three disciples at the Mount of Transfiguration. Where were the other nine disciples? We suppose Jesus had not prepared them for such a sight or that Jesus began to lay a unique foundation for the selected three.

Jesus taught and worked uniquely with diverse groups and individuals. So we see from the Scriptures many examples of differing ranks in the Kingdom: those who stayed behind, the multitude, the 70, the 12, and the three. Therefore, Jesus set a pattern for the present Kingdom of God.

The word "disciple" means "a disciplined one." They discipline their lives. A disciplined Christian is one who eagerly digs into the scriptures, who disciplines their walk according to what the Scriptures reveal to them, and who, by their spirit, rules their own soul and body. They hold their tongue and temper, forgive quickly, don't hold resentment, don't over-eat, and exercise and discipline both mind and body. They discipline themselves regarding their habits and thought life. What people say or do doesn't easily hurt their feelings. They are led by the spirit, ever learning and willing to walk in new truths that God reveals to them. They willingly submit to authority. Many Christians today love the gifts and blessings of God and cherish His love. But just expose them to a deeper Word that suggests a disciplined life style and they back off.

Think, for a moment, about well disciplined children. They obey and show respect to their parents and their elders and take on more responsibility as they mature. They eagerly learn and develop self-discipline and learn to control or discipline their own emotions and feelings. They actively seek the discipline and guidance of their parents—for it offers them guidelines or boundaries by which to live. Such children realize that parents are more mature and have most often developed sound judgment.

"And he turned him unto his **disciples**, and said **privately**, Blessed are the eyes which see the things that ye see: For I tell you, that many prophets and kings have desired to see those things which ye see, and have not seen them; and to hear those things which ye hear, and have not heard them." (Luke 10:23-34) Notice here that Jesus singled out His disciples, even privately, to impart blessings and teachings that the multitude and even the prophets before them didn't receive.

The book of Matthew further clarifies the above truth. "And the disciples came, and said unto him, Why speakest thou unto them in parables? He answered and said unto them, Because it is given unto **you** to know the mysteries of the Kingdom of heaven, but to **them** it is not given." (Matt. 13:10-11)

The "**you**" are the disciples, while the "**them**" are the multitude. What did the disciples receive that the multitude didn't? They received the private, deeper teachings, and the explanations of the parables. They walked and talked with Jesus day by day for three and one half years. They saw His miracles, His healings, and saw how He acted in all types of situations.

A disciple of Jesus today

A true disciple in the Kingdom of God keeps his mind open to receive new teaching, whether spoken or written, and will study it to see if it lines up with the Word of God. They will not hop from one church to the next because of doctrinal differences or other little things that might bother them.

Jesus didn't reveal Himself to the masses as He did to the twelve disciples or to the three on the Mount of Transfiguration. Remember He was as a human, yet as God. Neither is God a God without emotions, feelings, or expression. He is a God of personality, a multi-faceted Person who expresses Himself in millions of ways through a many membered body. Jesus is the visible expression of the invisible God. "Who being the brightness of his glory, and the express image of his person...". (Heb. 1:3) Jesus is the same yesterday, today, and forever. He was that image in his earthly ministry; He is that same image now in the hearts of believers and He will be in the future.

The words He spoke were spirit and life. He spoke from His heart. Consider the softness of His voice as He put a child on His lap. Or consider the compassion as He spoke to a blind man or the sternness as He drove out the moneychangers from the temple.

Today, a seasoned disciple of Jesus doesn't just read and meditate on the Scriptures, nor just accept its revelations, but **he hears the voice of the Lord Jesus Christ and obeys it.** Jesus Himself taught in John 10:3-4, "To him the porter openeth; and the sheep hear his voice: and he calleth his own sheep by name, and leadeth them out. And when he putteth forth his own sheep, he goeth before them, and the sheep follow him: for they know his voice."

If we hear His voice, then we hear more than mere words; we "hear" in our spirit the expression and sense or feel the deeper meanings behind the words. If the Scriptures are sharper than a two edged sword, (and they are) and Jesus' words are spirit and life, then those words reveal to us in their finest minute detail, a present reality, a present revelation for our very life. If the Scriptures are sharp enough to divide the soul and spirit, then we can discern in our spirit by the Word of God, which thoughts originate from our soul (or soulish realm) and which originate from our spirit. That two edged sword separates the soul and spirit not only in what we read and discern from the Scriptures but what is preached.

In order to hear His voice in the fullness, we must hear His voice corporately. If we isolate ourselves from the rest of the body, many of our own thoughts enter in and we are unable to distinguish the voice of God from our own thoughts. But as we come together corporately with the rest of the body, we can receive confirmation from the preaching, prophesy or witness of others as to what we hear from God. As for me personally, God also speaks to me through various versions of the Bible. We can also hear revelations of God from other members of the body.

We read in 1 Corinthians 1:5, "That in every thing ye are enriched by him, in all utterance, and in all knowledge." The Moffatt translation reads, "In him you have received a wealth of all blessing, full power to speak of your faith and full insight into its meaning."

Out from all parts of life emerges a birth process. If Jesus' words are life, then those words birth meaning to life and they will birth within us and through us a divine personality and expression that others may receive.

Jesus reveals Himself to us, letting us know not just the Word, but the feeling and expression of that Word. Jesus said that when the day of Pentecost came, the Holy Spirit would bring to their (the disciples) remembrance what was said. The accounts in the gospels cover only fifty some days out of the three and one half years of Jesus' earthly ministry. Can you imagine all that Jesus taught and showed them? "And there are also many other things which Jesus did, the which, if they should be written every one, I suppose that even the world itself could not contain the books that should be written. Amen." (John 21:25)

A very profound statement by Jesus was made when he said: "...Verily, verily, I say unto you, Except ye eat the flesh of the Son of man, and drink his blood, ye have no life in you. Whoso eateth my flesh, and drinketh my blood, hath eternal life; and I will raise him up at the last day. For my flesh is meat indeed, and my blood is drink indeed. He that eateth my flesh, and drinketh my blood, dwelleth in me, and I in him." (John 6:53-56).

Then a few verses later, John records in John 6:66, "From that time many of his disciples went back, and walked no more with him." They chose to no longer walk with Jesus. Here we see the distinction between those who continued to walk with Jesus and those who dropped out of the deeper teachings (a respect of persons). We see the same thing today. Many believers, satisfied with the loaves and the fishes, refuse to walk in the deeper things and deeper truths of God. As soon as they hear a deeper Word, or one that requires them to exercise discipline in their daily life, they sneak away or disappear and don't come back to church. Therefore, we distinguish between those who walk on with God and those who stay behind. Neither God nor the body of Christ forces that label upon them, but they choose themselves which path to walk.

If God was a respecter of persons in all things, including revealing and teaching the truth, then He would water down what He said so that all could understand and accept, and none would walk away. If Jesus was a total respecter of persons, then He would have either taught all people in parables or would have taught none in parables. Is not that the case today? Some understand at the parable level while others comprehend the deeper things of God. Where Jesus did show respect as to His teaching, He taught the multitude, His disciples, or the inner circle of three, each group on a level of their own understanding, regardless of their social or religious standing.

"For the earnest expectation of the creature waiteth for the manifestation of the sons of God" (Rom. 8:19). It's the sons of God who first know the mysteries of the Kingdom. and who are of the first order to help bring in others into the knowledge of God. For further study on the sons if God, read my book, "The Rising Son."

"Howbeit when he, the Spirit of truth, is come, he will guide you into all truth: for he shall not speak of himself; but whatsoever he shall hear, that shall he speak: and he will show you things to come. He shall glorify me: for he shall receive of mine, and shall show it unto you" (John 16:13-14).

The Holy Spirit came to a select group of people on the day of Pentecost. He initially came to each individual only through a Pentecostal experience. He reveals the Christ (not Himself) continually to those who seek the deeper truths and who listen to His voice. The corollary is that those believers without the Pentecostal experience, that is, those of the 30-fold realm, usually do not receive that same depth of guidance and revelation from the Holy Spirit.

"For the Holy Ghost shall teach you in the same hour what ye ought to say." (Luke 12:12) People with the power of the Holy Spirit, when they come before the people and powers of the world, are led by the Holy Spirit as to what to say. Those not led by the Holy Spirit are led by their natural mind. It's that simple. Therefore, you have a respecter of persons in this matter. It was future (**shall** teach you) at the time Jesus spoke this, but the Holy Spirit did come 50 days after the resurrection of Jesus. So it is now a present reality and it has been for nearly 2,000 years.

The Kingdom of God is a present reality but it is obvious that not all Christians follow all the rules of the Kingdom, nor do they live by all the principles of the Kingdom. In other words, all of us have some areas in our lives in which we do not conform to Kingdom principles.

Offerings Compared

How does God distinguish between the offerings of different people? "And Jesus sat over against the treasury, and beheld how the people cast money into the treasury: and many that were rich cast in much." (Mark 12:41) "For all they did cast in of their abundance; but she of her want did cast in all that she had, even all her living." (Mark 12:44) This widow had cast in all she had but the rich cast in only their surplus. Therefore God was displeased with the rich in how they gave. So here again, Jesus showed "respect of persons" when He contrasted the rich with the widow woman.

As for Cain and Abel, we read in Genesis 4:4-5, "And Abel, he also brought of the firstlings of his flock and of the fat thereof. And the LORD **had respect unto Abel** and to his offering: But unto Cain and to his offering he had not respect. And Cain was very wroth, and his countenance fell." In Hebrews 11:4 we read, "By faith Abel offered unto God a more excellent sacrifice than Cain, by which he obtained witness that he was righteous, God testifying of his gifts: and by it he being dead yet speaketh." God compared the offering of Cain with that of Abel. Therefore, He showed respect of persons.

We find in the Scriptures other examples of God showing favor to His people. "But Noah found grace in the eyes of the Lord." (Gen. 6:8) "But the LORD was with Joseph, and showed him mercy, and gave him favour in the sight of the keeper of the prison." (Gen. 39:21) God showed respect unto the children of Israel (Exod. 2:25) and Moses found grace in the sight of God. (Exod. 33:12) Mary likewise found favor with the Lord. (Luke 1:30) Thus, people like Noah, Joseph and Moses, God places in leadership.

"And when he was alone, they that were about him with the twelve asked of him the parable. And he said unto them, Unto you it is given to know the mystery of the kingdom of God: but unto them that are without, all these things are done in parables: That seeing they may see, and not perceive; and hearing they may hear, and not understand; lest at any time they should be converted, and their sins should be forgiven them." (Mark 4:10-12) "But without a parable spake he not unto them: and when they were alone, he expounded all things to his disciples." (Mark 4:34)

CHAPTER 11

▼

ARE YOU A LEADER OR A FOLLOWER?

What is a leader? Simply, it is a person whom people follow. Whether you lead a bible study of three people or lead a ministry of thousands, it matters not. Leaders may have certain abilities, whether inherent or God given in which people look to for leadership, whether projects, ideas or a wide variety of skills. Such are simple examples of a leader. Strictly speaking, especially in spiritual matters, we follow only those who follow Christ.

Do you hate to think of yourself as a follower? Or do you shrink from submitting to authority? Well, you can at least take comfort that you're not alone. Remember though that you can be both a follower and a leader at the same time. As a personal example, I have done a little amateur carpenter and concrete work. I didn't mind being a follower or a helper in these areas for a larger project for the local church or for its members. For carpenter work, I can be a follower or a leader. In a like manner, when I operate my computer, I either follow or lead, depending on the situation.

I call on certain brothers in the Lord for help and advice who are more expert in this area than I am, but I also give advice to others who are less knowledgeable on how to operate a computer.

In our Christian lives, we need to follow willingly, submitting to the direction and advice of others. At other times, we need to assert leadership roles of responsibility and teach others.

We may fear the thought of the responsibility that a leadership role in the Kingdom may require. Yet God may gradually or even suddenly change our heart so that we can accept that leadership role in our Christian walk. We often however, need to pass through a process to advance to the role of a leader. If you listen and obey the Holy Spirit, God will advance you accordingly.

You may not think of yourself as a leader, but in God's eyes, you might have great potential to be a great leader. You may not necessarily be a "formal" leader such as one in the five-fold ministry, Sunday School teacher, song leader or deacon. If you set an example by your godly Christ-like character and nature however, then you are a leader in character, for others will look up to you.

A person can't be a good leader however, until they first learn to be a faithful, dependable follower. They don't just walk into a new job and become the president of the company. If they are training to preach, they may first lick stamps, mail envelopes, take out the trash and care for the PA system in a church or ministry. Remember that Elisha followed Elijah a long time before Elijah passed the mantle to him and then God blessed Elisha with a double portion.

Those who aspire to leadership in ministry might learn some valuable lessons by studying the life of Elisha. Much took place between the time Elisha touched Elijah's mantle (1 Kings 19:19-20) and when he received the double portion of his spirit. (2 Kings 2:13) A leader must be patient in the development of his ministry.

Part of the story we read from 1 Kings 19:15-21 NKJV, "Then the LORD said to him: "Go, return on your way to the Wilderness of

Damascus; and when you arrive, anoint Hazael as king over Syria. "Also you shall anoint Jehu the son of Nimshi as king over Israel. And Elisha the son of Shaphat of Abel Meholah you shall anoint as prophet in your place. "It shall be that whoever escapes the sword of Hazael, Jehu will kill; and whoever escapes the sword of Jehu, Elisha will kill. "Yet I have reserved seven thousand in Israel, all whose knees have not bowed to Baal, and every mouth that has not kissed him."

"So he departed from there, and found Elisha the son of Shaphat, who was plowing with twelve yoke of oxen before him, and he was with the twelfth. Then Elijah passed by him and threw his mantle on him. And he left the oxen and ran after Elijah, and said, "Please let me kiss my father and my mother, and then I will follow you." And he said to him, "Go back again, for what have I done to you?" So Elisha turned back from him, and took a yoke of oxen and slaughtered them and boiled their flesh, using the oxen's equipment, and gave it to the people, and they ate. Then he arose and followed Elijah, and became his servant."

A leader, as Elisha was, willingly tells his family and friends that they intend to sacrifice their old lifestyle in favor of following the Lord. (v. 20) Elisha, showing the character of a leader, willingly followed Elijah a long time, doing menial tasks, often sacrificing wealth. A leader in the ministry must know how to slay with the sword (1 King 19:17; Heb. 4:12), that is, apply the Word of God, as a two edged sword, with wisdom and discernment. A good leader in the Kingdom must never be too proud to serve other ministries. They will help him in his ministry. Do not misunderstand. We do not suggest that one serve just to get help in return. Lastly, a good leader knows that to aspire to great heights in God will require sacrifice, revelation and insight.

Paul declared, "I press toward the mark for the prize of the high calling of God in Christ Jesus. Let us therefore, as many as be perfect (Gr: complete), be thus minded: and if in any thing ye be otherwise minded, God shall reveal even this unto you." (Phil. 3:14-15)

In the above verse, Paul wrote, "I press toward the mark." If all are equal in the Kingdom, or all will receive equal rewards, either now or in the next life, why should we bother to press on? We might as well sit back and let others do all the work, all the believing, and all the exercising of faith! If some received a high calling, then there must also be lower callings or ranks. The above verse indicates that God separates those who are perfect ("complete"—Phil. 3:15) from those who are not. In another scripture, "**As many** as are led by the Spirit, they are the sons of God." (Rom. 8:14) The phrase "As many" indicates that not all are led by the spirit.

If all were equal in the Kingdom, it would mean that the slothful, the lazy, and those lacking ambition would inherit equal gifts and blessings or places of leadership in the Kingdom. Similarly, they would receive the same level of revelation from the Lord. We know this isn't true. Romans 12:11 warns, "Not slothful in business; fervent in spirit; serving the Lord;" Here we speak about life in the Kingdom now, and in the years to come and about the future on the other side of the grave, however you might describe or define that.

Some people, like the Pharisees, seek high positions so that others will look up to them. But those higher positions require more responsibility of leadership and example. People in those positions must lead a cleaner, holier life, lest those who look up to them might stumble. "But whoso shall offend one of these little ones which believe in me, it were better for him that a millstone were hanged about his neck, and that he were drowned in the depth of the sea." (Matt. 18:6)

How does a person accept other people who seem to walk at a different level in the Lord than they do? They don't look down on those who they feel are below them in any area of their spiritual life, for that is arrogance. On the other hand, they don't look up to those they feel dwell above them, for then they may become jealous or envious.

Concerning ministry gifts, "And God hath set some in the church, first apostles, secondarily prophets, thirdly teachers, after that miracles, then gifts of healings, helps, governments, diversities of tongues." (1 Cor.

12:28) V. 29-30, "Are all apostles? are all prophets? are all teachers? are all workers of miracles? Have all the gifts of healing? do all speak with tongues? do all interpret?"

Notice the word "some" in verse 28. This indicates that God calls some into certain types of ministry and gifts and others not. The obvious answer to the questions in verses 29-30 is "no." If not all members of the Kingdom function in the five-fold ministry or as leaders, then some serve as laity, followers or subjects in the Kingdom. The sons of God, who assume their proper role in leadership, help to bring this order to the Kingdom of God.

God distinguishes between the ministry and the laity. "And he gave some, apostles; and some, prophets; and some, evangelists; and some, pastors and teachers; For the perfecting of the saints, for the work of the ministry, for the edifying of the body of Christ:" (Eph. 4:11-12) In this last verse, most versions omit the comma after "saints." To rephrase these verses, the task of the five-fold ministry is to perfect or bring into maturity the saints, whom will have the task of ministering to others.

God warned: "…Touch not mine anointed, and do my prophets no harm." (1 Chron. 16:22) I have seen first-hand many times when someone spoke falsely or acted against a man or woman of God, and then fallen into serious problems down the road. I believe this is a form of judgment from God. It's one thing to speak wrongly of one person to another but to tear down another ministry of God on national radio or TV or in books and magazines distributed nationally are to multiply the sin 100-fold.

In the New Testament, we find that the Apostle Paul or the Apostle Peter, along with the other leaders, were certainly not the same as the laity. They not only received more revelation and authority from God but also more responsibility. The ascension gifts, that is, the apostle, prophet, evangelist, pastor, and teacher, however, are not titles to use as positions of influence but are ministries, with specific functions or callings within the body of Christ.

We might add that God calls some to be followers. Faithful, dependable followers, ones who strive to move forward in the Kingdom, need not feel inferior. God needs them to fulfill the functions of His subjects.

Leadership role

The Holy Spirit reveals the Christ (not Himself) continually to all those who seek the deeper truths and listen to His voice. Yet such believers God most likely places in positions of leadership. On the other hand, to those who do not seek the deeper truths (often the mysteries), He will not reveal Himself. These mysteries of God are frequently the simple things, not the complex.

In the Old Testament, God chose the people of Israel above all other. Now the Church is God's chosen instrument to take the gospel to the world, the leadership that brings others into the Kingdom. .

If God confers kings and priests in the Kingdom, then as kings whom do they rule over? There has to be subjects for them to rule. These subjects include the natural born children coming into maturity and those coming into the Kingdom, the 30-fold realm.

In the account of the centurion (Matt. 8:5-10), the centurion realized the parallel between his submission to authority and the submission of Jesus to the authority of God. Furthermore he recognized the parallel between the authority delegated to him in the natural realm to the authority delegated to Jesus over sickness in the spiritual realm. See Chapter 12 for further study on this subject. Some people may advance further or faster in the Kingdom, including a role of leadership, because they willingly submit to authority, whether of ministry or of God. These people simply can then exercise authority over the things and circumstances that may come against them, whether these circumstances come from the outside or from thoughts in their own mind.

Jesus warned, "Take heed therefore how ye hear: for whosoever hath, to him shall be given; and whosoever hath not, from him shall be taken even that which he seemeth to have." (Luke 8:18)

Now verse 21 from the same chapter in Luke says, "And he answered and said unto them, My mother and my brethren are these which hear the word of God, and do it." The margin in the NKJV states for "seems to have" means "thinks that he has." Notice in these two verses we have examples of a distinction between those that hear the Word and do it and those who don't hear the Word. Again, those who hear the word are more likely to advance in leadership. Jesus explains the parable of the sower. To "take heed on how you hear" means to not be like those on the wayside, not to be like the ones who have no root or be like the ones who are choked with the cares of the world. We must be careful how we express this parable.

Some would say that since God is no respecter of persons, all receive equal revelation of the Word of God. Not so. The seed is the Word of God. The Word is sown, but all do not receive it equally because of how they hear it. The fault lies not in God or the incorruptible seed but in how each one hears the Word or in the condition of their heart.

Leadership qualities.

First we must recognize the divine image of God which resides in each other, whether we lead or follow. In today's complex society, leaders become vulnerable, whether in the local church setting or as believers in the workplace, in a large part because they must make choices. Yet the responsibility to make choices distinguishes leaders from followers. You may ask, "How do leaders become vulnerable?" One way is that people want a leader to act as a peer, yet expect them to stand apart. That is, people want their leaders to be infinite gods instead of finite human beings. The average person doesn't like others to know he or she is vulnerable, yet vulnerability is a key to effective leadership.

The leader's capacity to trust in God depends on the nature of his or her belief in God and the degree to which he or she can cultivate such a relationship. Leaders who trust God involve themselves in His presence on a daily basis. Leaders, as humans, lack perfect knowledge, that is, they do not have perfect knowledge at the time of decision, so must acknowledge the sovereignty of God in all things.

Faith in God provides leaders a guide to the future. "By faith Abraham, when he was called to go out into a place which he should after receive for an inheritance, obeyed; and he went out, not knowing whither he went"(Heb. 11:8). These heroes of faith of Hebrews, Chapter 11 had confidence in the future God had laid out for them.

Leaders who have placed their trust in God can actually take more risks than those who believe the future depends upon human reasoning. Such leaders step into the future with confidence in spite of the unknown, because the Spirit of God, rather than their own natural mind, leads them. Leaders must be able to develop visions and value systems for themselves, the local church and the Kingdom of God. Such things however, must originate from recognition of the past, present, and future. Biblical faith, the assurance of the resurrection of Jesus Christ and the knowledge of Christ in them, the hope of glory, furnishes the leaders with such a guide.

God's calling on each of us as leaders or followers enhances our whole lives, not just a career or position in an organization or local church. Listening to God is therefore imperative for effective leadership. From the Scriptures, for example, God called Noah to build an ark while Enoch's call was to walk with God. .

Effective leaders have developed their faith, a faith not in their careers, their local church, in the environment, or in the future but faith in a person, the Lord Jesus Christ. Faith cometh by hearing and hearing by the word of God. The apostle Paul came on pretty strong concerning faith, "...for whatsoever is not of faith is sin." (Rom. 14:23). Furthermore we need to know who God is and who we are, have faith for our calling and exercise faith in our work or position in the Kingdom of God, whether we happen to be operating in or outside of our local church.

He Who Has an Ear

Some people may not advance in rank or to a position of leadership in the Kingdom because they have lost some of their (spiritual) hearing. Jesus said, "He who has an ear, let him hear what the Spirit says to the churches..." (Rev 2:7 NKJV) It's apparent that he is talking about our spiritual ear and it also obvious that not everyone has a spiritual ear to hear.

What happened to their ear? Possibly one or more of several things: (1) Their spiritual ear has been cut off. (John 18:10) (2) Their ear became dull of hearing. (Heb. 5:11) (3) Their spiritual ear isn't yet developed. (Heb. 5:12-14) (4) Not all hear all things spiritually, but instead they try to hear or understand some things with their natural mind. And the natural man is totally incapable of hearing what the spirit says. (1 Cor. 2:14) (5) Some turn away their ears from the truth. (2 Tim. 4:3-4) " Some are as Ezekiel described, "...hear your words, but do not do them." (Ezek. 33:31) (6) God's appointed leaders will hear deeper truths than others will. (Exod. 33:11; Amos 3:1; John 15:15) (7) Some refuse to let God develop their hearing, for within every believer resides the germ of spiritual hearing. I believe people in this group get more pleasure or satisfaction out of hearing or trying to understand the natural rather than the spiritual meaning of their circumstances, and (8). Many Christians feel content to remain in the 30 or 60 fold or in some beaten path within those realms.

Let's go back to number (1) above and look at it a little closer. This scripture deals with Peter cutting off the servant's ear. Peter was trying to defend his concept of the identity of Jesus and his concept of Jesus' mission on earth. Now let's apply that in the spiritual. We become defensive when people want to take away our Jesus, that is, take away our concept of His identity, where He came from, or the reality of His virgin birth. Has He come again or did He ever leave? If He hasn't come, when will He come and in what form? Will He have a literal sword in His mouth riding on a literal white horse? Will he have nail scarred hands? Does He still heal the sick and perform miracles?

Some people become defensive when you take away some of the literal meaning of the Scriptures. With others, if you take away the cross with Jesus still hanging there, they become defensive. To them He remains the suffering servant. They view Jesus as either a historical or a future figure. Instead, they should perceive the reality of the present Jesus Christ, in the now, living and abiding in His saints. When someone tries to take their concept of Jesus away, they become defensive and attempt to cut off the other's (spiritual) ear. With this loss of hearing they can't advance in the Kingdom.

How do people cut off our ear? They do this when they speak words of condemnation, or find fault. They might tell us that our idea or project would never work, that we look sick, that our ideas are all wrong. They may show us Scripture to prove their point. If we spend much time with people who speak a lot of negative words, this can also hinder our ability to hear the Spirit. Some people become jealous and envious of our position in God so they "cut off our ear" by telling us we are in error or have missed God. In short, they don't want us to hear so well spiritually.

We realize that it is God, rather than man, who develops our spiritual ear and eye (Pr. 20:12). But as outlined above, certain things can hinder that growth. Some believers refuse to heed what they hear the Lord telling them to do. This could range all the way from calling a certain Christian brother or sister on the phone, to a change in career, church home, housing or in basic attitudes. Those who refuse to yield to dealings of the Lord certainly won't advance in the Kingdom or advance in leadership or at least not until they begin to obey the Lord. They will be left behind in rank or position (not salvation).

Jesus likened a man who hears God's word but refuses to do anything about it, as one who builds his house on the sand. "And every one that heareth these sayings of mine, and doeth them not, shall be likened unto a foolish man, which built his house upon the sand." (Matt. 7:26 See also

Neh. 9:35) "Therefore to him that knoweth to do good, and doeth it not, to him it is sin." (Jas. 4:17)

Peter Walks on the Water

You remember when Jesus and Peter walked on the water (Matt. 14:22-33). This account teaches many practical lessons but for now we will limit ourselves to those relating to rank. In verse 22, "...He (Jesus) sent the multitude away. Four classes of people appear in this account. First, the multitude, whom Jesus sent away. In this case, they dwell in a lesser realm or level of spiritual understanding. He sent them away, not in rebuke or in condemnation, but to protect them from the storms of the sea. The sea speaks of humanity while the storms symbolize the manifold troubles of humanity. (Isa. 57:20; Rev. 13:1; 17:1) In a similar way today, God protects the multitude in the world from many of the storms of life.

The second group of people, the eleven disciples (those other than Peter), Jesus now tested. Just barely keeping afloat on the sea of humanity, they see a figure through the fog and darkness, symbolizing problems of the natural realm. It was Jesus walking on the water and they thought it was a ghost (A phantom; no relation to the Holy Ghost). A phantom has no substance. Many Christians today are like the disciples. They fail to see or believe the reality of Jesus, that is, the Spirit of Jesus living within them, Christ in them, the hope of glory, Jesus walking on water, walking above the troubles of the sea of humanity, walking above their own personal problems.

Such Christians don't grasp the reality that they can live in victory through the Christ within them. They perceive a Jesus in the distance, unreachable, out in the sky, one who walks or exists in a different dimension, a different time frame—either past or future—than the present storm or condition in which they now live.

The average Christian doesn't realize their true identity in Christ, nor do they grasp the reality of their reconciliation to Christ. (2 Cor. 5:18) He or she doesn't comprehend the wisdom of God within him or her through

Christ (1 Cor. 1:30), the fullness of Christ (John. 1:16; Eph. 1:23), nor the reality of an inheritance in Christ Jesus (Col. 1:12). They don't realize that we are in Him and that we have been given all things that pertain unto life and godliness and a partaker of His divine nature. (2 Pet. 1:3-4)

The third person in the account was Peter. He longed to penetrate that higher dimension. He reached out to Jesus, challenging Him, "If it is you Lord, bid me to come." The other disciples no doubt heard Jesus say, "Come" by their natural ears. But Peter listened with His *spiritual* ear and heard Him say, "Come." It's when we hear by our spiritual ear that the Word of God energizes us and are then able to move into that spiritual realm. Only Peter really heard. Each person has to hear from God on his or her own. Peter represents the class of people who will listen with their spiritual ear and heed the call.

Peter stepped out in faith when he stepped out on the water. The first thing we need to do to walk on water is to get out of the boat, out of our comfort zone. We too can step out in faith. Jesus invites us to come from where we are spiritually, to where He is (spiritually). When we emerge out of that storm we are in, we rise to a higher dimension in Christ. As we walk by faith, one step at a time, we trust not in our walk nor in our ability to hear spiritual truths, but in Jesus Christ. We walk from a place of our natural mind, a place of relative safety (in the boat, yet still in the storm), to a higher place of (spiritual safety) **above** the storm. We don't wait for the storm to pass, but walk through or above the storm.

The fourth person in the account was Jesus. He, of course, never faltering, constantly walks in the spiritual or heavenly realm. (John 3:13) Yet he reached down to Peter, picked him up, restored him to the spiritual realm (on top of the water), for they, together walked back to the boat. Those Christians in this realm identify, not with the multitude, nor with the eleven disciples, nor even with Peter, but they identify with Jesus. They, by the power of the Holy Spirit, stretch out their hand (speaks of ministry and service) to those who are falling and restore them to the spiritual realm. Walking on water, above the storms, they are led by and energized by the Holy Spirit.

Jesus walked on water as a man, not as God. "The works that I do shall ye do"—speaks of an equality with Jesus. (John 14:12) Though Jesus remained in the heavenly realm, He manifested Himself in a lower realm, to the men in the relative safety of the boat. He ministered on their level, yet He did not compromise His position of the higher dimension. He didn't try to coax the other disciples to try to walk on the water, nor did He condemn them for not trying. Again, we see here four ranks or levels of leadership in the Kingdom: the multitude, the eleven, Peter, and Jesus.

Before a person can rule others, he must first be able to rule his own spirit (Prov. 16:32; 25:28). Next, each member of the Kingdom must submit to the proper order or rulership in the church. 1 Peter 5:1-4 refers to the elders in the church but this can apply to anyone moving in leadership. Those who rule properly will receive a crown of glory.

Order in the Kingdom

Order in the Kingdom of God begins with the proper order of man himself in his relationship with God. God has a love for all creation and He has not given up on that which He has created. "For I know the thoughts and plans that I have for you, says the Lord, thoughts *and* plans for welfare *and* peace, and not for evil, to give you hope in your final outcome." (Jer. 29:11 AMP)

Before a person can rule others however, he must first be able to rule his own spirit (Prov. 16:32; 25:28). Next, each member of the Kingdom must submit to the proper order or rulership in the church. 1 Peter 5:1-4 refers to the elders in the church but this can apply to anyone moving in leadership. Those who rule properly will receive a crown of glory.

Order in the kingdom includes numerous aspects. The apostle Paul outlines in 1 Corinthians, chapters 12 and 14, order in the local church or assembly concerning the use of spiritual gifts. God gave nine gifts to the church to help build the foundation of the Kingdom, as outlined in 1 Corinthians 12:8-10. Yet, there are some believers who teach that these gifts are old order. As far as other aspects of order, Paul writes to Timothy concerning the qualification of a bishop (1 Tim. 3), the duty of servants (1 Tim. 6), rules in administering reproof, and how to treat elders, women, and widows in the local church.

The Scriptures state several instructions concerning order in the local church. (See 1 Cor. 7:17; 11:34; 14:23, 40; Titus 1:5.) Also see Titus chapter 1 for discussion on the ordination of elders and qualifications of ministers.

In the Hebrew culture, a child was nursed and brought up by the mother until it was 12 years old when the father began to train the child. We know that a woman represents the Church. In the New Testament church the apostles and leaders preached meat (solid nourishment of the Word of God) at the temple, then the people met in homes to break bread, that is, to break down what the apostles had taught. (Acts 2:42, 46).

We should follow that same order in the local assemblies today. It's the duty of the pastors and leaders to minister the strong meat, the deeper Word (not milk) to the church. We know in the natural, a woman nursing a baby has to have good solid food in order to nurse. Therefore, the local church's responsibility is to feed the milk of the Word to the new members. That is, the church and its mature members ought to be teachers, feeding the young or new converts and helping break down the Word or bread. We have to do more than hear the Word. We must share it with others. The people need to study and meditate on the Word themselves, not depend on the minister to spoon feed them.

A good leader of a group of 50 believers has the gift to discern the details of problems of individual members and has divine wisdom to guide and direct them to solve such problems as well as other beneficial guidance for their daily lives. When a pastor has an active assembly of 50, he can do this. But when the local assembly grows to 100, 500 or more members, then much of that individual attention is lost.

Don't feel inferior if you are a leader or minister of a small group. Such people are absolutely necessary in the Kingdom of God. They see those details that those leading thousands cannot see or have been called to do.

Paul wrote to the Romans: "And so all Israel shall be saved: as it is written, There shall come out of Sion the Deliverer, and shall turn away ungodliness from Jacob." (Rom. 11:26) Is this for only the natural Jew? NO! He writes in verse 32, "For God hath concluded them all in unbelief, that he might have mercy upon all."

God has plans for us. He is omnipotent. "Yea, truth faileth; and he that departeth from evil maketh himself a prey: and the LORD saw it, and it displeased him that there was no judgment." (Isa. 59:15) "The Lord saw it." He is mindful of His creation; thus He knows our circumstances.

It's not the people outside of us, the raging nations that are our enemies. It's our own internal realm, the kings within our own mind, those that war against the will of God that Jesus Christ subdues. "For he must reign, till he hath put all enemies under his feet." (1 Cor. 15:25) These kings we put down are the kings of fear, doubt, unbelief, procrastination, anger, lust, over-eating, idolatry, criticism, condemnation, hatred, jealousy, selfishness, strife and other works of the flesh, anything that tries to rule in our mind. Once we rid ourselves of these kings, Jesus Christ can then rule as King, first in the mind and heart of the sonship company, who then rule with Him in the world.

We know that we need a Deliverer who saves us from our sin. Yet, He not only removes us from sin, but also banishes all ungodliness from us, and then takes us and forms a new creation, one with His divine nature, one in His image. This is order in the Kingdom of God.

CHAPTER 12

▼

OUR STOREHOUSE IN THE KINGDOM PART 1. TREASURES IN HEAVEN

What treasures do we lay up or store in heaven or in the heavenly realm? Those things we give to the Kingdom include anything we give to further the work of the Kingdom, whether money, time or talent, really our attitude and mind. That money may help build buildings, buy music supplies, help members in need or may be used for any ministry that lines up with the Word of God. Spiritual treasures include love, joy, peace, longsuffering, gentleness, meekness, and the gift of helps. We lay in store these treasures.

Jesus taught, "Do not lay up for yourselves treasures on earth, where moth and rust destroy and where thieves break in and steal; but lay up for yourselves treasures in heaven, where neither moth nor rust destroys and where thieves do not break in and steal. For where your treasure is, there your heart will be also." (Matt. 6:19-21 NKJV)

Treasures laid upon earth, on the other hand, both tangible and intangible, satisfy only our soul (mind, will and emotions) and body—they will rust—they last but a fleeting moment. Anything that satisfies only our earthly, lower nature falls into this category.

The word "rust" (Gr.: *brosis*) from the above verse means to eat or to devour. It eats away or oxidizes the object to nothing. Moth damage refers to woolen material riddled by the larvae of the moth, becoming so fragile the material has become worthless. The larvae thus speak of the power of destruction, almost without notice, but eventually destroying the object. Wool relates to labor in the flesh or sweat; so in the earth realm, all products of the flesh are destroyed.

Ezekiel describes the garments of the priesthood, which specifies that they wear no wool. (Ezek. 44:17) Today this means that a priest (that is all believers) is not to minister from the flesh.

The word "lay" comes from the Greek word *thesaurizo, which* means to lay or store up, (akin to *thesauros*, which is a treasury, a storehouse, and a treasure. James, speaking of the rich, tells us, "Your riches are corrupted, and your garments are moth-eaten. Your gold and silver are corroded, and their corrosion will be a witness against you and will eat your flesh like fire. You have heaped up treasure *(thesauroizo) in* the last days." (Jas. 5:2-3 NKJV)

The Amplified version expresses verses 4-5 as follows, "[But] look! [Here are] the wages that you have withheld by fraud from the laborers who have reaped your fields, crying out (for vengeance), and the cries of the harvestores have come to the ears of the Lord of hosts. [Here] on earth you have abandoned yourselves to soft (prodigal) living and to [the pleasures of] self-indulgence and self-gratification. You have fattened your hearts in a day of slaughter."

Here in James we see the extreme negative or results of not laying or storing treasures in heaven or in the heavenly realm. If we accumulate treasures by fraud, self-indulgence or for earthly pleasure, that activity will witness against us.

In Matthew 19:21 (NKJV) Jesus advised the rich young ruler, "...If you want to be perfect, go, sell what you have and give to the poor, and you will have treasure in heaven; and come, follow Me.". The Amplified reads, "...if you would be perfect [that is, have that spiritual maturity which accompanies self-sacrificing character], go and sell what you have and give to the poor, and you will have riches in heaven..." "But when the young man heard that saying, he went away sorrowful, for he had great possessions." (Matt. 19:22 NKJV)

Paul wrote to Timothy regarding those that are rich in this world, admonishing them not to trust in uncertain riches but in the living God, and Part of his exhortation is as follows: "**Laying up in store** for themselves a good foundation against the time to come, that they may lay hold on eternal life." (1 Tim. 6:19) If we are born from above, we have that eternal life. It's a gift. In contrast, we have to put on immortality. (1 Cor. 15:53)

Unfortunately many of us want to hang on to our "treasures" when the Lord instructs us to give something for the Kingdom. We cry, "That's mine, that's mine! That's my hard-earned money. Can't I have a little pleasure out of life?" We also tend to want the credit for what we do for the Kingdom. "I prayed and God healed him." Or "I prayed and the Lord moved." "I did this; I did that for the Lord." But we must believe that the Lord has our best interest at heart when He leads us, even when we give our "treasures," and we shouldn't care if people recognize us or not.

We have this treasure in earthen vessels. (2 Cor. 4:7) We are that earthen vessel. The vessel is not the treasure; it merely contains the treasure, the living Jesus Christ. We (that is, the body of Christ collectively), are the temple of the Holy Spirit. (1 Cor 6:19 NKJV) The temple therefore contains the glory, but is not the glory itself.

God's plan and purpose, that is, in the heavenly realm, has no element of time. God created time yet He dwells outside of it. But the manifestation of His plan in the earth realm is governed by time, for time becomes an integral part of man. Among other things, central to God's plan were the birth, life, burial and resurrection of the Lord Jesus Christ.

Christ always existed. His manifestation, however, as Jesus of Nazareth, in the visible realm, was by appointed time. (Isa. 7:14, 9:6; Luke. 1:31; John 1:14) God simply dropped Jesus of Nazareth into the pages of the history of man. Likewise, when we release our treasures into the heavenly realm here in the earth, then God can take and use them to fit into His plan.

What or where is heaven?

If we are to lay up treasures in heaven, then we need to know what or where heaven is. "Heaven" is an extremely broad subject that we can't fully discuss here. Suffice it to say however, that heaven is many things, but heaven isn't out in the sky. It's not a geographical place and it's not tied to some future time. Jesus dwelt in the heavenly realm while He walked the earth. (John. 3:13) Paul was caught up into a heavenly realm, one of at least three heavens. His feet never left the planet earth, but his spirit was caught up in that third heaven. God made the heaven(s); they aren't material. Heaven is a state of being, a condition of our mind.

Jesus emphasized, "I go to prepare a place for you..." (John 14:2) "Who has gone into heaven and is at the right hand of God..." (1 Pet. 3:22 NKJV) That place He is preparing is not a physical place out in the sky but a spiritual dimension within each believer, a state of being where we can communicate with God. We can partake of that now. God dwells in the saints and God dwells in the heaven, so heaven resides within us. (John 17:21-23; Matt. 6:9; 1 John 3:24)

If you are a believer of the Lord Jesus Christ, then you are now seated in a heavenly place in Christ Jesus (Eph. 2:6.), even though you may not know how to operate in that realm. Where is that? "Far above (spiritually, and in authority, not geographically) all principality, and power and might, and dominion, and every name that is named, **not only in this world (age)**, but also in that which is to come" (Eph. 1:21)

What is commonly called the Lord's prayer, which is in reality the disciples prayer, is cited in Matthew 6:9-13. Jesus didn't mean it as a prayer to memorize or to repeat exactly as it is, but He taught to pray *in this manner*. "Thy kingdom come,...on earth as it is in heaven..." He is teaching us to pray that all the attributes, characteristics, principles, power and direction of the heavenly realm will take control and authority over our situation upon the earth, even those of an earthy dimension, the events of our everyday life. This is now, present tense. We aren't waiting for some future manifestation of a physical Jesus, except as He appears now in His many-membered body, for this to happen.

Through this prayer, we affirm that the rulership, authority and law of the Kingdom which prevails now in the heavenly realm will prevail over each situation and phase of our lives in the earth, even our very attitude, as our mind is renewed day by day (Rom. 12:2).

What is God's will in the heavenly realm? God's will is for the Kingdom of God to manifest Himself in and through a people. This manifestation expresses itself in His very image, nature, likeness, rule and power and in the fulfillment of His purpose in their everyday lives. By the faith of God, that purpose has already come to pass in the heavenly realm. Through time, our prayers, and the hand of God it then manifests in the natural realm. It has been manifested since the day of Pentecost, is now still manifesting and it will continue to manifest. —Past, present and future—that is the Kingdom of God coming to earth as it is in heaven. (Again, for a detailed discussion on this manifestation of God through the sons, see my book "*The Rising Son.*")

Jesus tells us to pray in this manner: "Thy kingdom come...as it is in heaven." This statement is not passive, nor does it tell us to beg God to do something. Rather, it's a statement of fact of what has already been done in the heavenly realm. Such a prayer or statement means something much stronger than just turning the situation over to God. In controlled anger, we stomp our foot down and proclaim to the situation, "God's rulership has authority and His will is in control here and it will prevail."

Let's turn again to the scripture where Jesus instructed us to, "Lay up for yourselves treasures in heaven..." When you lay them up in heaven or place them in the heavenly realm, then God will see to it through His divine wisdom, authority and rulership, that He will direct those treasures to help fulfill His purpose in our lives and of those affected by that treasure. We aren't just laying up these treasures in some future heaven, some future time that will yield no present benefit. We don't wait for some nebulous concept that we must wait till we "die and go to heaven" (there is no such concept in the Bible) to receive the benefits. Remember that you enter the Kingdom of God by birth, not by death. It is like depositing into a savings account that begins to pay dividends now in this life but also in our next life on the other side.

So many Christians, concerning the above verse, believe they can't have any thing in this life, but if they work hard to please God, they can have it in the next life. As for the non-believer or people in the world, they either think there is nothing beyond this life so live in pursuit of pleasure, excluding anything of God. Or they feel that if by chance they live halfway righteous, God may reward them in the next life. These concepts are not scriptural.

When we lay up our treasures, we release control and rulership over that treasure, whether it is tangible or intangible, and give it to God. Jesus (re: Matt. 6:9 Thy kingdom come...) is saying that in particular situations and areas in our lives we ought to pray for God's will rather than our will to prevail. This will then lead to fulfillment of His purpose in our lives.

For the born-again believer, the Kingdom of God has already come in many areas of their life, for the principles of the Kingdom operate in and through them, in their earthly body and in their earthly environment. Those attributes of the Kingdom of Heaven, including God's rulership and God's will are in a real way, in a storehouse for us to use now!

We Have Redemption

Speaking of Christ, we read, "In whom we have redemption through his blood, the forgiveness of sins, according to the **riches of His grace.**" (Eph. 1:7)

The word "riches" comes from the Greek word *ploutos* meaning that abundant **store** from which we receive God's lovingkindness and glory. *Ploutos* is used in the singular of material riches (Matt. 13:22; Mark. 4:19 and others), but for our discussion, speaks of spiritual and moral riches. *Ploutos* (riches) is used in Romans 2:4 as possessed by God but extended toward man—"riches of His goodness and forebearance and longsuffering..." Ephesians 2:7, "That in the ages to come He might show the exceeding **riches of His grace** in his kindness toward us through Christ Jesus." So great are the treasures stored up for us in the Kingdom that Paul uses the word *ploutos* (riches) five times in the book of Ephesians.

From Ephesians 1:7, "In Whom we have redemption" is in the present tense and duration in action. Thus redemption is an abiding fact from the past, through the present and into the future (Word Studies in the Greek New Testament, Vol. 1, Wuest). This redemption through His blood is the "forgiveness of sins" (remission: KJV) which means letting them go as if they were never committed.

Now this forgiveness is "according to the riches of His grace." "According to" comes from the Greek word *kata* meaning "down" or speaks of domination or control. The degree of this forgiveness is thus dominated or controlled by the riches *(ploutos)* or wealth, and abundance of God's grace. That abundant grace is infinite in proportion. Thus the forgiveness is complete and unchanging.

"Wherein he hath abounded toward us in all wisdom and prudence." (Eph. 1:8) The word "abounded" *(perisseuo)* means to exceed a fixed number or measure. God's grace was manifested to us in superabundance. From Wuest Vol. 1, p 42, "It (His grace) is more than enough to save and keep saved for time and eternity, every sinner who comes to God in Christ Jesus." "That at the name of Jesus every knee should bow, of things in heaven, and things in earth, and things under the earth; and that every tongue should confess that Jesus Christ is Lord, to the glory of God the Father." (Phil. 2:10-11)

The word "redemption" (Eph. 1:7) here comes from the Greek word *apolutrosis* which means a releasing on payment of a ransom. It is used in referring to deliverance from physical torture (Heb.11: 35), deliverance from the guilt of sin, (Rom. 3:24) through the redemption that is in Christ Jesus"; (Col. 1:14), the forgiveness of our sins, indicating **both** the liberation from the guilt and doom of sin and the introduction into a life of liberty (W.E. Vine).

From Hebrews 9:15 (NKJV) states: "For the reason He (Christ) is the Mediator of the New Covenant, by means of death, for the **redemption of the transgressions**, under the first covenant..." Redemption (*apolutrosis*) is also used as the deliverance of the believer from the presence and power of sin and of his body from bondage or corruption. "And not only they, but we also who have the firstfruits of the Spirit, even we ourselves groan within ourselves, eagerly waiting for the adoption, **the redemption of our body.**" (Rom. 8:23 NKJV)

Access to the Authority of the Kingdom

Another blessing that God has given to us from His vast storehouse of treasures is access to the authority of the Kingdom of God. "And these signs shall follow them that believe; In my name shall they cast out devils; they shall speak with new tongues; They shall take up serpents; and if they drink any deadly thing, it shall not hurt them; they shall lay hands on the sick, and they shall recover." (Mark 16:17-18)

The word "believe" from the above verse speaks not of one whom is barely saved but of one whom believes in and walks in the deeper truths of God. "Serpents" speak of evil spirits; they shall not hurt the believer. The term "deadly things" refers to false doctrines and teachings. The believer can hear them but it won't hurt him.

"Speak with new tongues" means they will speak a new word, which comprises three aspects: (1) a change in our vocabulary. When we are born again, we quit cussing and speaking so much negative talk. We begin to speak by faith. If God gave you a new tongue, why would He not also give you a new mind to go with it, a mind that would think of spiritual things, and a mind that moves by faith. (2) Through the baptism of the Holy Spirit we begin to speak a heavenly language (in tongues), and (3) We speak the tongue of the learned, a deeper word. Three parts of this last aspect include (a) a witness for Christ, (b) speaking a heavenly language of spiritual things and (c) the gospel is revealed to the believer so that they have a deeper understanding of the gospel; as a result, they will speak a deeper (new) word.

Now we come to an important point regarding teaching. "And Jesus came and spake unto them saying, All power (NKJV- authority) (Greek: *exousia*- delegated authority or delegated influence), is given unto me in heaven and in earth. Go ye therefore, and **teach** all nations, baptizing them in the name of the Father, and of the Son, and of the Holy Ghost: Teaching them to observe all things whatsoever I have commanded you: and, lo, I am with you alway, even unto the end of the world (age)." (End of carnal self, not the end of the planet earth). (Matt. 28:18-20) This baptism does not infer water baptism but a baptism of teaching. The subject of this passage is teaching, not water baptism. In other words, Jesus first received authority (delegated from God) and in turn delegated that same authority to the believers.

In another example, Jesus told Peter, "I shall give to you the keys of the kingdom of heaven; and whatever you bind on earth (forbid to be done), shall have already been bound (forbidden to be done) in heaven; and whatever you loose on earth (permit to be done), shall have already been loosed in heaven (permitted to be done)" (Matt. 16:19 Wuest Expanded). By giving the keys of the Kingdom, Jesus was giving Peter and present members of the Kingdom the authority and the rulership of the Kingdom. The Lord Jesus has granted us the authority to act in earth and heaven will back us up.

The authority of the centurion

Let's turn next to the account of the centurion whose servant was sick and ready to die. (Luke 7:2) We pick up the words of the centurion directed to Jesus in verse 7, "Wherefore neither thought I myself worthy to come unto thee: but say in a word, and my servant shall be healed. (8) For I *also* am a man *set* under authority, having under me soldiers, and I say unto one, Go, and he goeth; and to another, Come, and he cometh; and to my servant, Do this, and he doeth it. (9) When Jesus heard these things, he marveled at him, and turned him about, and said unto the people that followed him, I say unto you, I have not found so great faith, no, not in Israel. (10) And they that were sent, returning to the house, found the servant whole that had been sick."

The Amplified reads (v. 8), "For I also am a man **daily** subject to authority; with soldiers under me..." Wuest: "For I **also** am a man whose position in life places him under **constant authority of others,** have at the same time soldiers under me. And I say to this one, Go at once, and he goes, and to another, Be coming, and he comes, and to my slave, do this and be quick about it and he does it."

The centurion recognized the parallel between his delegated authority and chain of command and that of Jesus. More specifically, he recognized that Jesus was not only under the authority of God, but through that submission to God, would have divine authority (delegated from God) over the sickness which was obviously of a lower order. How was that authority exercised? By speaking a word. "**Just speak a word** and my servant will be healed."

Again, we wish to emphasize from the principles set out in these verses that the authority of the believer isn't the concept of a gift, a grant or a proclamation. Rather it is delegated authority that flows like a chain of command. The believer constantly subjects himself to Jesus Christ, the Higher authority, in order for him (the believer) to exercise his authority. Again, this authority is a treasure stored in the heavenly realm, available now for any believer willing to walk out the principles.

In this case, the spoken word generated the response to the line of authority. The centurion **spoke** to his soldiers while Jesus *spoke* to the disease or the person with the disease. Both the centurion and Jesus constantly subjected themselves to a higher authority. Why can Jesus delegate authority to believers over sickness and circumstances? It's because He was and is now subject to the authority of God.

Jesus said, "The words that I speak unto you, they are spirit, and they are life." (John. 6:63) His words of substance released an energy force that commanded authority over the lower realm of sickness. In the same way, the words we speak are an energy force. Life speaks of a higher order than death. The sickness emerged from the death realm, a realm outside of God, a lower form or level of existence.

In his book *The Prophetic Community,* Earl Paulk writes about the Roman centurion, how he got and understood his authority, and the chain of command, then Paulk states, "In our case, God put man on the earth to subdue it and take dominion over it (see Gen. 1:28). But we can't give orders until we have learned to take them. We can't be in that position of power and authority until we have been under authority. Under whose authority do we serve? The authority belongs to the One who earned it—the Eternal King of the Kingdom, Jesus."

The spoken word—that is how Jesus demonstrated the authority over satan, over demons, by words of divine wisdom to the Pharisees, to sickness and to the death of Lazarus and of two others.

Jesus sent the 70 out with His authority and with specific instructions: "Go your ways: behold, I send you forth as lambs among wolves. Carry neither purse, nor scrip, nor shoes: and salute no man by the way. And into whatsoever house ye enter, first say, Peace be to this house. And if the son of peace be there, your peace shall rest upon it: if not, it shall turn to you again. And in the same house remain, eating and drinking such things as they give: for the labourer is worthy of his hire. Go not from house to house. And into whatsoever city ye enter, and they receive you, eat such things as are set before you: And heal the sick that are therein, and say unto them, The kingdom of God is come nigh unto you. "(Luke. 10:3-9)

Now verse 16, "He that heareth you heareth Me, and he that despiseth you despiseth Me; and he that despiseth Me despiseth Him that sent me."

Here's another example of the delegated authority Jesus gave us: "Behold, **I give you the authority** to trample on serpents and scorpions, and over all the power of the enemy, and nothing shall by any means hurt you." (Luke 10:19 NKJV).

Speaking of Nicodemus, we read in John 3:2, NKJV, This man came to Jesus by night and said to Him, "Rabbi, we know that You are a teacher come from God; for no one can do these signs (KJV: miracles) that You do unless God is with him." The word "sign" comes from the Greek *semeion* (akin to *semaino,* to give a sign and *sema, a* sign) and refers to miracles and wonders as a **sign of divine authority.**

Jesus acknowledges the authority given to Him again in the following scripture as He was praying to His "Father, "....Father, the hour has come. Glorify Your Son, that Your Son also may glorify You, **as You have given Him authority over all flesh**, that He should give eternal life to as many as You have given Him." (John. 17:1-2 NKJV) Here the Greek word *exousia* (authority) refers to the power or rule of government, the power of one whose will and commands must be obeyed by others (W.E. Vine).

Remember, "Thy kingdom come..." (Matt. 6:9) We are to reign as kings—we have been given the authority to exercise rule and dominion over situations in the earth. That is now, not just in the distant future! Otherwise, Jesus wouldn't have us to pray "in this manner."

The delegated authority granted to us isn't something we try to take and run with, doing as we will. We don't grasp it just to inflate our own ego, exploit for selfish gain, or to satisfy our own flesh. Rather, it's an authority in which we constantly subject ourselves to the authority of

God, just as Jesus constantly subjected Himself to God while He was on the earth. We must not break that chain of command.

Then with that authority the believer can take command over the things of the earth realm, starting with their own earthly actions, their own flesh, sicknesses, thoughts, those things of a lower order than our spirit. I believe the reason so many Christians don't see results of their spoken word of authority over their situations and circumstances is because they don't submit to the authority of God in their lives. James 4:7 illustrates this principle well. "Submit yourselves therefore to God. Resist the devil, and he will flee from you." The second part of the Scripture won't work unless you obey the first part. It's also because we speak so many negative, idle words and so much exaggeration in our conversation.

From the book of Daniel we read, "But the saints of the Most High shall take the kingdom, and possess the kingdom for ever, even for ever and ever" (Dan. 7:18). This does not mean that we take the Kingdom by exercising our authority. Before we can do that we must be strong enough to possess it, and worthy to inherit it. If we try to take it before God gives us that authority, we are usurpers, not inheritors.

If I tell you tell you that I intend to give you $100 but you come and take it out of my house before I give it to you, you are a thief. If you worked for a company and the head of the company told you he intended to make you department head, but you took over the authority of the department head before the time, you would be a usurper. In the same manner, we as individuals, don't yet have all the authority and glory of the Kingdom of God. Yet when a person properly has God's authority in any given area of their life, and properly exercise that authority, it will work.

Circulating in some churches now, a false teaching implies that we can't have the possessions of God now, in this lifetime. They are reserved, so they say, for some future time, for another people (the natural Jew), or for another dimension.

God has given each of us unique talents and abilities so that we can in turn multiply these gifts to help advance and further the Kingdom of

God. We are not to hide these treasures under a bushel or bury them, but put them to use. In the parable of the talents, to the faithful servants who demonstrated that they were trustworthy by multiplying their talents, their master encouraged them, "Well done, good and faithful servant, you were faithful over a few things, I will make you ruler over many things. (Matt. 25:21).

Most of us want to advance in the Kingdom but we have placed the Kingdom of God lowest priority in our activity and do not use the talents the Lord has given us. . But we choose to do everything our own way. If we would begin to live and walk out daily what we say we believe on Sunday, we would turn the world upside down.

CHAPTER 13

▼

OUR STOREHOUSE IN THE KINGDOM
PART 2. POWER TO FINISH THE COURSE

The power we need to finish our course (our race) or our divine mission in life resides within every believer in Jesus Christ. We can tap into this power, now present in our spiritual being, at any time. We should have the confidence that to this end God is working in us, energizing us. Paul wrote to the Philippians, "Being confident in this very thing, that He which hath begun a good work in you **will perform it** until the day of Jesus Christ." (Phil. 1:6) "The Lord will perfect that which concerneth me..." (Ps. 138:8).

Paul indicates to Timothy in the following Scriptures that he now has finished the course. "I have fought the good fight, I have finished the race, (KJV: course) I have kept the faith. Finally, there **is laid up for me the**

crown of righteousness, which the Lord, the righteous Judge, will give to me on that Day, and not to me only but also to all who have loved His appearing (Gr: *epiphano,* manifestation, to appear, become visible)" (2 Tim. 4:7-8 NKJV). This appearing speaks of Christ's manifestation IN His saints.

Notice the definite article "**the** good fight," which indicates the good fight which each Christian wages. It's compared to a Greek wrestling match, strength against strength. Paul also states, "I have finished my course." The word "course" comes from the Greek word meaning a race-course. "Finished" is in the perfect tense, which means a past completed action with present existing results. I believe Paul felt that he was at the end of his life—finished the race—finished all that God had purposed for him.

The Lord began His work in us in our mother's womb. "For you did form my inward parts. You did knit me together in my mother's womb. I will confess and praise you, for you are fearfully wonderful *and* for the awful wonder of my birth! Wonderful are Your works, and that my inner self knows right well. My frame was not hidden from You, when I was being formed in secret *and* intricately *and* curiously wrought (as if embroidered with various colors) in the depths of the earth [a region of darkness and mystery]. (Ps. 139:13-15 AMP.)

Philippians. 2:12-13 in Wuest's Expanded Translation reads, "Wherefore, my beloved ones, as you always obeyed, not as in my presence only, but now much more in my absence, carry it to its ultimate conclusion (likeness to the Lord Jesus) your own salvation with a wholesome, serious caution and trembling, **for God is the one who is constantly putting forth His energy in you,** both in the form of your being desirous of and of your doing His good pleasure."

The NAS version of v. 13 reads, "...for it is God who is at work in you, both to will and to work for His good pleasure." The Amplified puts it this way, "...[not in your own strength] for it is God who is all the while effectively at work in you—**energizing and creating in** you the power and desire—**both** to will and to work for His good pleasure *and* satisfaction *and* delight."

If we stay tuned to the Spirit of God within us, He will direct our ways and give us the power to do what He desires us to do. One of His highest goals for us is to come into the image of Jesus Christ. When our desire begins to line up with His desire, then He will continue to direct our will. Our own selfish desires will eventually fall by the wayside.

From Wuest, Vol. 2, p 74: The word "worketh" (KJV) in the Greek means "to energize, to work effectively" It is this desire to do the good pleasure of God that is produced by divine energy in the heart of the saint as he definitely subjects himself to the Holy Spirit's ministry. It is God, the Holy Spirit, who energizes the saint, making him not only willing, but also actively desirous of doing God's sweet will. **But He does not merely leave the saint with the desire to do His will. He provides the necessary power to do it.**"

It's not so much that the Lord convicts us of our earthly, fleshly desires, those that satisfy only our soul (mind, will and emotions), though He will do that. It's more that He gives us those fresh, spiritual, holy desires, those that bring life and that line up with the Word of God. These desires then supersede those arising from the earth plane or our soul realm.

Crowns in store

There are two different words in the Greek translated as "crown" (KJV). One is *diadema,* which is always the symbol of kingly imperial dignity, and is translated "diadem" in the Revised Version (Rev., 12:3; 13:1). (W.E. Vine).

The other word, *stephanos,* means that which surrounds, as a wall or crowd and denotes (a) a victor's crown, the symbol of triumph in the games or some contest such as wrestling, a reward or prize, and (b) a token of public honour for distinguished service (W.E. Vine). The *stephanos* was a symbol of victory, therefore, a victor's crown, while the diadem is a royal crown.

In Philippians 3:7-14 Paul, by example, instructs us by key elements how to live a Christ-like life. He declares "that I may know Him and the power of His resurrection." (v. 10) That speaks of a relationship. Concluding in verse 14, "I press toward the mark for the prize of the high calling of God in Christ Jesus." Again, contrasted with a race, the athletes receive a corruptible *stephanos* (crown) of oak leaves that soon withers, while the overcoming Christians receive a *stephanos,* an incorruptible crown.

James assures us, "Blessed is the man that endureth temptation (testing); for when he is tried, he shall receive the victors crown (*stephanos)* of life" (Jas. 1:12). This crown of life is not a free gift for all believers but is reserved for only the victors or overcomers. Paul explains to the Corinthians the analogy of a race and the resulting prize. "Do you not know that those who run in a race all run, but one receives the prize? Run in such a way that you may obtain it. And everyone who competes for the prize is temperate in all things. Now they do it to obtain a perishable crown, but we for an imperishable crown." (1 Cor. 9:24-25 NKJV)

Paul continues, "But I discipline my body and bring it into subjection, lest, when I have preached to others, I myself should become disqualified." (1 Cor. 9:27 NKJV) (KJV translates the last phrase: "become a castaway")

The Greek word for "castaway" is *adokimos*, meaning one disqualified, not allowed to compete for the crown. He is disapproved, so rejected from present testimony, with loss of future reward. This reward that Paul speaks of doesn't refer to eternal salvation but to a victor's crown won through Christian service. It's this crown that is stored up in the Kingdom. Again, it's in "storage" for our present life, not something future.

Our True Identity

We have an identity that comes directly from God and is thus "stored" for us in the Kingdom or heavenly realm. First of all, we are created by God and are unconditionally loved by God. Then if we are born from above, we can also respond to Him in an obedient relationship and know Him intimately. If we are born from above, we have a myriad of identifying characteristics, each significant. Each one of us must know in our heart and mind just who we are. It's an identity that can't be lost or diminished. Put another way, our identity, when we are in the proper position to receive it, is in store for us to partake of **here and now**, not just in the future. All the related benefits of our identity are also in "store."

For example, in our identity, we are the righteousness of God in Christ (Gal. 3:38); we are Abraham's seed (Gal. 3:29); we are the salt of the earth (Matt. 5:13); we are a joint heir with Jesus Christ (Eph. 3:6); a king and priest (Rev. 1:6); a new creature (2 Cor. 5:13); a temple of the Holy Spirit (1 Cor. 3:16); more than a conqueror (Rom. 8:32); God's workmanship (Eph. 2:10) and part of the True vine (John 15:1, 5). This is just the beginning. For further insight, read the first chapter of Ephesians. We have the potential to become the elect (Col. 3:12); and to become an overcomer (1 John 5:4).

If we are born again, the scriptures declare, as He is, so are we (1 John 4:17). He (Jesus Christ) is who we really are. Our real person or our real identity is not what other people or we see from the outside. The real us is the Christ (which means "anointed") on the inside. The real us is the inner man, the spiritual man. (Eph. 3:16) 1 Corinthians 6:16-17 explains, " What? know ye not that he which is joined to an harlot (an intimate relationship without commitment) is one body? for two, saith he, shall be one flesh. But he that is joined unto the Lord is one spirit."

Paul declared, "For me to live is Christ" (Phil. 1:21). Romans 6:6 states that our old man is crucified with Christ. That was our old identity. The only thing man can do exactly is mathematics. It's an exact science. You know that 2 x 2 equals 4, whether you are in Peoria, Hong Kong or Moscow, in the first century or now. Paul wrote to the Christians in Rome, "Likewise reckon ye also yourselves to be dead indeed unto sin, but alive unto God through Jesus Christ our Lord." (Rom. 6:11) The word "reckon" here from Strong's 3049 means "to take an inventory." Reckon is simply a mathematical term, a fact. It simply is a fact that if your are born again, then you reckon you are dead to sin and you also reckon that your old man or adamic nature was crucified. From verse 6, "Knowing this, that our old man is crucified with him, that the body of sin might be destroyed, that henceforth we should not serve sin."

We don't strive to work up faith to believe it or struggle to walk it out or wait for some future time. That has nothing to do with it. It is a fact that your old man was crucified with Christ. To reckon is like balancing a checkbook. You simply match your account with the bank's statement. Now you accept what the Word of God says. It's when we don't realize that our old man is dead that we have problems. Our identity is in Jesus Christ. That's the real you, the inner man.

We discussed elsewhere the importance of fellowship with other believers. It is through this personal intimacy with them and with the Lord Jesus Christ that we maintain our humanity. Conversely, when we cut ourselves off from such fellowship, we diminish who and what we are. We maintain our humanity by interaction with other believers. It is really the Christ in us who interacts with the Christ in others. We are a part of His body. To cut ourselves off, we become less than whole. "For the body is not one member but many." (1 Cor. 12:14)

It's important to see ourselves as we really are—our identity with Christ. So many Christians see themselves as weak and helpless, no better off than those of the world. They fail to realize our strength dwells in the Lord and in His might. (Eph. 6:10).

Let us examine another aspect of your identity: Quit trying to be somebody else. Just be the person God created you to be.

Don't covet somebody else's ministry or gifts. For one thing, you don't know what they have been through to arrive where they are. Jeremiah 29:11 (NKJV) assures us, "For I know the thoughts that I think toward you, says the LORD, thoughts of peace and not of evil, to give you a future and a hope." Quit trying to live in the past. Your future, if in God, has so much more for you than anything of your past.

Fallen man seeks his identity not in who he is but in what he does. The adamic man is ashamed of who he is, so he hides behind fig leaves (coverings, masks). He identifies with what he does and his feeling of success concerning what he does (possessions he accumulates), and what others think of what he does or of his success. He seeks their approval concerning what he does, not who he is. The adamic man wants to be liked, but he fears rejection by others, so he covers himself with those fig leaves so that others cannot see his faults and his failures.

I may ask someone, "Who are you?" And they will say, "I am an office worker, or a factory worker, a salesman, a teacher, a truck driver, a retail clerk, a minister, a waitress, a farmer, a father, a mother." That is actually not who you are, that is what you **do**.

Most people continue to transfer that false identity (performance orientation) to their relationship with God. They seek God's love by working or by performing for God, by going through rituals, that is, rituals sanctioned by their local church or by their denomination, by their particular field of business or employment, or by their own mind, always striving to do better so that God will love them more.

But our true identity, that is, the one that comes from God through Jesus Christ, isn't just a "handle" to our name but a multi-faceted force or attribute in which we can tap into. We can claim this attribute in order to strengthen our walk in the Kingdom and therefore overcome obstacles across our path as we advance in the Kingdom. When we know by our spirit who we are, then we can lay claim to our inheritance and God's promises in the Kingdom.

We should identify with the love that comes through God and what He did for us. When we know in our heart that love of God and properly receive it, then we no longer depend upon the approval of others for our identity.

Yet our identity means much more than a smorgasbord of scriptural truths and claims. When we know our true identity by the power of the Holy Spirit, we have an important key to walking in total freedom in the Kingdom, free from the bondage of "performance orientation." Furthermore, our identity helps us to give meaning to life.

Who are you? Some may say, "I am a failure." That is not who you are, that is only your concept of the relative success of your performance, not a failure of whom you are. We may feel that we are a failure in our career, in our finances, in the goals we have set for ourselves, in our family, in our personal relationships, in getting rid of bad habits or in developing good habits, in serving God, and the list can go on.

One may make promises to themselves. For example, one who has had an unhappy childhood for any number of reasons may vow to do anything they can to make themselves and other people happy. Yet when they are unable to do that, they feel guilty, so they feel that they are a failure. Again, such a person concentrates on what they do rather than who they are. God created man to be human BE-ings, not human DO-ings.

Some may feel they are a failure because they cannot overcome sin in their life. The problem may be that they try to do it in their own strength. They may not fully realize that Jesus died for their sins. We do not condone sin, but state a truth. If they have the baptism of the Holy Spirit, He also gives them that extra power to overcome both sin and the flesh and the means to appropriate that power.

Some may say, "I am a workaholic," or "I am an alcoholic," or "I am a drug addict." That isn't who they are, that is what they do or a habit they have become enslaved to. Someone may say, "I am a diabetic". Again, that isn't who they are; it's only a manifestation of symptoms in their body.

The Christian life isn't free of failures, disappointments, tribulation and trials, but when we know fully in our heart (by the Holy Spirit) who we are, that is, our true identity, our identity with Jesus Christ, these trials don't overwhelm us. We can draw on the reality of our identity (in that storehouse of treasures) to give us strength during these trials. Failure, by the way, is not an enemy but a teacher. You can either let failure discourage you or you can learn from it. Thomas Edison failed in thousands of experiments before he found the right filament for the electric light bulb, but he never gave up.

Yet with these inevitable failures along life's path, no one is ever defeated until defeat has been accepted as a reality in one's mind. So keep yourself (your mind) free from all fear of defeat and it will never become a reality in your life.

The average Christian believes that going through life without tribulations and problems is a mark of always being in favor with and in the will of God. This is far from the truth! Just read the scriptures about the trials of Abraham, of David, Peter, Paul, Elijah, and others. Read about tribulation in the Epistles. Our trials are but minor bumps on the road along our journey in life and should not command a significant place in our thought life.

We deserve afflictions, but afflictions don't come to us because we deserve them. They come to us as God sees our need for processing. We must quit trying to figure out what is happening to us and know that God is working out His will in our life (Phil. 2:13).

From his prison cell in Rome, Paul wrote, not about his imprisonment, but about Christ. He wrote, "...For when I am weak, then I am strong." (2 Cor. 12:10). He recognized his weakness but didn't identify with that weakness, but with the Christ who gave him strength. He boasted, "I can do all things through Christ which strengtheneth me" (Phil. 4:13).

Failure doesn't change who we are one iota when we know our identity is in Christ. But if our identity is in our performance—in what we do—rather than in who we are—then failures, which are inevitable, will almost without a doubt lead to a loss of self esteem and self worth. Paul knew who he was and lived out the reality of that knowledge. How could he have written what he did (the 1st and 3rd chapter of Ephesians, for example), if he had not had the experiential knowledge of Christ working and living in him? For example, "That the God of our Lord Jesus Christ, the Father of glory, may give unto you the spirit of wisdom and revelation in the knowledge of him..." (Eph. 1:17)

After the fall, Adam and Eve found their identity in what happened to them. Adam blamed Eve and Eve blamed the serpent. They became victims. In reality, a person is victimized by circumstances, (which does not change their true identity), but they choose by their own wrong attitudes to look upon themselves as a victim and thus wrongly identify themselves as a victim. A vast difference exists between being victimized and being a victim. Man blames circumstances on his condition and thus justifies any antisocial behavior or he blames previous circumstances (being victimized) on his failures in business or in his personal life.

The victim says, "I am not responsible for what I do because of what happened to me—because of my race, my nationality, my childhood, my family, because a drunk driver caused an accident to my family, or a business partner ran away with my money, or of crop failures on my farm, or I came from a broken family". The victim feels that he is a pawn of fate. In contrast, we are victimized by circumstances.

Concerning our perception of ourselves, let me quote from "The Cross and the Glory, Part 2" by Bob Klein, "Our perception of ourselves in God's perfecting process may be quite limited. What we see as a minor detail may be seen by God as a major stronghold. We're looking at the tip of the iceberg while God sees all that is submerged under the water. We've sometimes thought that major things are dealt with first, perceiving these to be the open sins of the flesh, obviously inappropriate for Christians. It may seem then that as we grow, God is just working on minor details. I think just the opposite is true, that God in his patience and mercy deals tenderly with us at first and later, as we grow in grace and are able to bear it, he goes after the foundations of these strongholds in the depth of our wicked hearts."

God's Unconditional agape love

We don't usually think of God's love as something stored in the Kingdom and it certainly is unique. God's love isn't confined to the Kingdom, for His love knows no boundaries and has no limitation. God is love. Yet love isn't something God has but love is Who He is, His very nature.

"God so loved the world that He gave his only begotten Son." (John 3:16) God loved the world, all mankind. "That He gave his only begotten Son" is an expression of His love. He gave the best He had. That act was based not on who we are but on who He is. Jesus Christ gave Himself, His very life, in an act of agape love. God's agape love doesn't depend upon what man does or doesn't do for man can't earn God's love.

We read in 1 John 4:7-10, "Beloved, let us love one another: for love is of God; and every one that loveth is born of God, and knoweth God. He that loveth not knoweth not God; for God is love. In this was manifested the love of God toward us, because that God sent his only begotten Son into the world, that we might live through him. Herein is love, not that we loved God, but that he loved us, and sent his Son to be the propitiation for our sins."

God doesn't love us because He expects us to love Him in return. In a similar way, you love another person not because of who they are or who you are or that you expect love in return, but because of God's love coming from the Christ within you. Sometimes we may not feel God's love arising from within us but we determine to obey the commandment to love one another.

When it comes a time that we need to lay down our life for our brethren, which is what agape love is, then we have that quality of agape love, God's love, within us. (1 Pet. 1:22-25; John 13:35) It's in our storehouse.

Agape love originated with God. God's love for man was not born out of a need of His or because He was lonely, but because of Who He is. Otherwise He would be incomplete. God's love isn't based on the idea that some day we will become lovable or come fuller into His image. It isn't based on our desire to live a better life. Nor is it based on any performance of ours, our degree of holiness, our dedication or our Kingdom work. God's love isn't based on our demonstration of love to Him or to our fellow man. God's love for us isn't based on how well we keep the law or the rules of our local church.

God therefore loves us by His free choice. He doesn't "need" to love to fulfill Himself. Neither does He need our love. This statement may shock you. But if God is waiting for our love to make Himself complete, then God isn't God.

Traditional teaching and thinking has distorted God's love in many ways. So many of us have come to think of God as a harsh taskmaster who is ready to punish us for every false move. Or some believe that somehow God's love must be earned through works—trying to be more holy or feeling they would receive more of God's love if they prayed or read their Bible more. At the other end of the spectrum, certain circles teach that God's love is so great, that He looks the other way on sin, which He never punishes or chastises. Such teaching isn't scriptural.

Now, an important point related to our present discussion. We don't have to "check our storehouse" each day to see if God's love is present, to see if maybe we have goofed and God somehow is withholding His love from us for some period of time. But we must believe that He loves us, and have assurance in our heart of His unconditional love. Jesus Christ passed the test and the results are "put in our storehouse." When we believed, God sent the Holy Spirit to live and abide in us. It's He who will assure us of God's love. It's that intimate knowledge of God's love from which we can "draw" from our "storehouse."

The Glory from the Heavenlies

Jesus declared, "And the glory which thou gavest me I have given them; that they may be one, even as we are one." (John 17:22) "Whereunto he called you by our gospel, to the obtaining of the glory of our Lord Jesus Christ." (2 Thess. 2:14) "For it became him, for whom are all things, and by whom are all things, in bringing many sons unto glory, to make the captain of their salvation perfect through sufferings." (Heb. 2:10) "That ye would walk worthy of God, who hath called you unto his kingdom and glory." (1 Thess. 2:12)

Contrary to what we imagined in the past, we don't go to a glory land or to glory. There is no scriptural basis for this concept. Glory comes to us, and is revealed in us. We experience glory as a present treasure here on earth. We now partake of that glory. Peter wrote, "The elders which are among you I exhort, who am also an elder, and a witness of the sufferings of Christ, and also a partaker of the glory that shall be revealed." (1 Pet. 5:1)

Let us look at the prayer of Jesus in John 17 concerning that glory in us. "And all mine are thine, and thine are mine; and I am glorified in them." (John 17:10) And in John 17:22, "And the glory which thou gavest me I have given them; that they may be one, even as we are one...:" Referring to being joint heirs with Christ, Paul writes in Romans 8:17, "...that we may be glorified together." "When Christ, who is our life, shall appear (be revealed), then shall ye also appear with him in glory." (Col. 3:4)

The glory of God is the visible manifestation of His attitude, nature, character, love, justice, righteousness and mercy. (Jer. 9:24) God now shines His glory in the relationships and contacts of the daily lives of the spirit filled Christians so that others can see what God is like. How is this glory related to laying up treasures? It's a quality that originates in the heavenly realm but a quality that God helps us to develop today, in this life. It's true that God will reveal more and more glory in the future. But the associated substance of that glory is a treasure we can have right now. It's a treasure in our storehouse from which we can now draw.

      *   *   *

Recommended Reading

Tony Campolo, *Following Jesus Without Embarrassing God* (Word Publishing 1997)

Kingsley Fletcher, *I have Seen the Kingdom* (Creation House 1998)

Thomas Keating, *The Kingdom of God is Like...*(Crossroad Pub. Co. 1997)

Bob Klein, *The Cross and the Glory, Part 1 & Part 2,* (Self Published.)

Peter J. Leithart, *The Kingdom and the Power* (Presbyterian and Reformed Publishing Company 1993)

Earl Paulk, *The Prophetic Community* (Treasure House, Imprint of Destiny Image 1995)

David Ravenhill, *For God's Sake, Grow Up* (Destiny Image Publishers Inc. 1997)

Kelly Varner, *Prevail* (Revival Press 1982)